rockschool®

POPULAR MUSIC THEORY

The *essential* guide for rock & pop musicians

GRADE 6 TO GRADE 8

www.rockschool.co.uk

rockschool®

POPULAR MUSIC THEORY

The *essential* guide for rock & pop musicians

GRADE 6 TO GRADE 8

Published by Rockschool Ltd. © 2015
CATALOGUE NUMBER: RSK011502
ISBN: 978-1-908920-68-3

PUBLISHING

WRITTEN, COMPILED & EDITED BY
Charlie Griffiths, Stephen Lawson, Simon Troup, Jennie Troup and Nik Preston

ART DIRECTION, COVER DESIGN, LAYOUT & ILLUSTRATION
Philip Millard | *www.philipmillarddesign.com*

COVER ILLUSTRATION
Adam Hill | *www.velcrosuit.com*

ADDITIONAL CONTENT & PROOFING
Prof. Joe Bennett, Simon Niblock, Jonathan Preiss, Stuart Slater, Mike Stylianou, Mary Keene, Stefan Redtenbacher, Owen Bailey, Chris Bird, Becky Baldwin, Ronan MacDonald and Philip Henderson

EXECUTIVE PRODUCER
John Simpson

SYLLABUS

SYLLABUS DEVISED BY
Charlie Griffiths, Stuart Slater, Prof. Joe Bennett, Simon Troup and Jennie Troup

SYLLABUS CONSULTANTS

Anna Cook, Joanna Taman, Rachael Meech and Mike Stylianou

PRINTING

PRINTED AND BOUND IN THE UNITED KINGDOM BY
Caligraving Ltd.

DISTRIBUTION

EXCLUSIVE DISTRIBUTORS
Music Sales Ltd.

CONTACTING ROCKSCHOOL

www.rockschool.co.uk
TELEPHONE: +44 (0)845 460 4747
EMAIL: info@rockschool.co.uk

CONTENTS

WELCOME

Congratulations. Either you've worked your way through Rockschool's *Popular Music Theory: Debut to Grade 5* and are ready for more, or you're an improving musician with a grasp of the theory basics and want to take your knowledge to the next level.

Popular Music Theory: Grade 6 to Grade 8 will act as a primer for the more sophisticated music theory covered in Rockschool's higher grade books, and will familiarise you with the musical concepts you'll need to master in order to pass Rockschool's Popular Music Theory Examinations. While the more in-depth ground we're covering here is orientated towards candidates taking those particular exams – as well as providing an accessible, structured guide to help tutors who are teaching the syllabus – the content will be useful to anyone taking Rockschool's instrumental exams, too. Plus there's no doubt it will also come in handy in many real-world scenarios you're likely to encounter as a working musician, long after you've passed your exams.

As you journey towards an appreciation of musical notation, becoming familiar with various scales, chords and time-signatures, you'll be steadily honing your analytical skills and improving your understanding of the most popular rock and pop styles and their instruments.

When you feel ready, it's now easier than ever before to enter Rockschool's Popular Music Examinations – just visit the website at *www.rockschool.co.uk/enter-online* and follow the quick and easy sign-up process.

MUSIC NOTATION

The longer you explore a subject, the more the study turns to looking at things that are seen less often. This chapter covers some of these more exotic topics – double sharps and double flats, double-dotted notes, odd note groupings and, finally, the 64th note. Sometimes however, given the right combination of key, style and complexity, you may find pieces of music making heavy use of this notation – so be prepared!

DOUBLE SHARPS & FLATS

The purpose of double sharps and double flats is to alter notes which have already been sharpened or flattened by the key signature; this often occurs when non-diatonic chords are introduced. For example, if you write out a D♯ minor chord (D♯ F♯ A♯) in the key of B, no accidentals are required because the F♯ is already in the key. If a D♯ major chord is required, you need to raise the 3rd by a semitone. The most obvious way to do this would be to raise the F♯ to G, producing the requisite notes of the chord, D♯, G and A♯. However, the problem with this is that intervals of a 3rd must always be spelled out using every *other* alphabetical letter – and G and A are consecutive. Using every other letter looks tidier on the stave, too: if a triad has its root note on a line, the 3rd and 5th intervals should also be on a line. Similarly, if the root note is on a space, the 3rd and 5th should be, too.

The solution is to sharpen the F♯ again so it becomes 'F double sharp'. F double sharp sounds exactly the same as G natural – the two are simply spelled differently. The double sharp is indicated on the stave below as a small '𝄪' placed before the note.

Below is an example that uses a double flat (♭♭). The first chord shown, G♭, is chord IV in the key of D♭. If a minor version of this chord is required (IVm), the 3rd (B♭) is lowered by a semitone (to B♭♭). Although B double flat and A natural sound the same, the B double flat spelling places the 3rd neatly in the space between the G♭ and D♭.

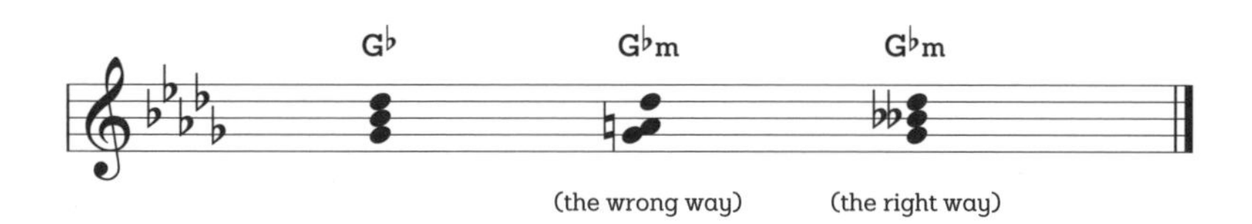

SMALL SUBDIVISIONS

You can divide each beat of the bar into any fraction by using subdivisions. You will have previously divided beats into smaller units, from quarter notes, to eighth notes, to eighth-note triplets to 16th notes. Now you will learn how to divide those notes into even smaller divisions.

16TH-NOTE TRIPLETS

THE 16TH-NOTE triplet is twice as fast as the eighth-note triplet and divides each beat into six equally spaced notes. When counting eighth-note triplets, it is helpful to vocalise the phrase by counting '1 & a 2 & a', etc. When we double the notes to 16th-note triplets, it becomes more difficult to vocalise due to the higher rate of notes. One approach is to use a six-syllable word which naturally rolls off the tongue (e.g. 'biodiversity').

16th-note triplets can be written in two ways. The first is to arrange the 16th notes into groups of three then place a bracket with a number '3' beneath each group (this is most commonly used when a group of three 16th notes is beamed with an eighth note). The second way is to bracket the notes into groups of six (sextuplets) and place a number '6' in the middle. Although the following two bars look different, they sound exactly the same.

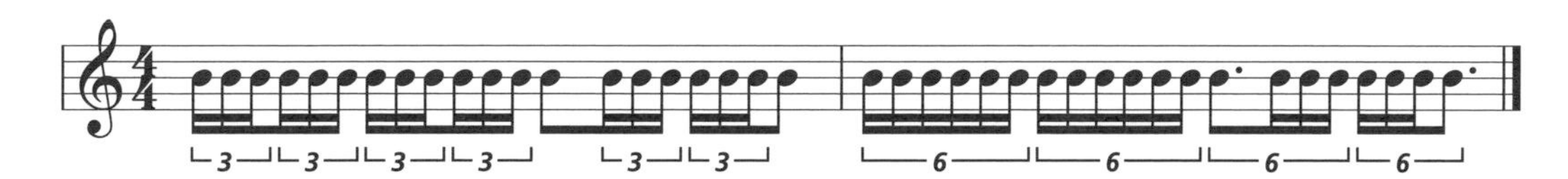

32ND NOTES

ALSO KNOWN as a demisemiquaver, this subdivision produces eight, evenly-spaced notes per beat. The notes are drawn similarly to 16th notes but are beamed together with three lines rather than two. In order to make the notes easier to read, each group of eight 32nd notes is split into two groups of four with a single beam connecting them. The second half of the bar shown below illustrates how 32nd-note rests can be grouped with 32nd notes.

64TH NOTES

ALSO KNOWN as a hemidemisemiquaver, this subdivision produces twice as many notes as a demisemiquaver (16 evenly spaced notes per beat). These are beamed together with four horizontal lines. For the sake of clarity each beat is split into two groups of eight with a single beam connecting them. The second half of the bar below shows how 64th-note rests can be grouped with 64th notes.

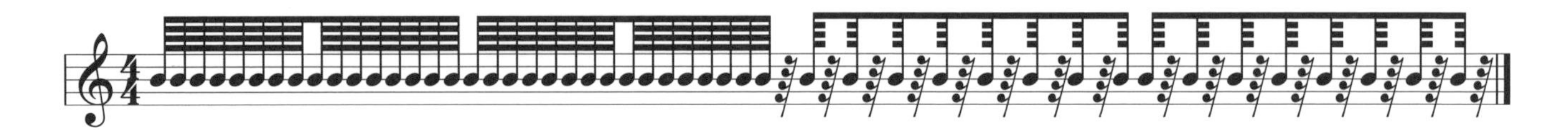

DOUBLE DOTS

TO UNDERSTAND double-dotted notes, let's take a step back to remind ourselves of what a dot does to a note. Think of the dot itself as being worth half the value of whatever precedes it. If you attach a dot to a four-beat note, the dot is worth another two beats (the combined total will be six beats, i.e. 4+2=6). If you attach a dot to a note worth half a beat, the dot is worth another quarter of a beat (the combined total will be three quarters of a beat: $\frac{1}{2}+\frac{1}{4}=\frac{3}{4}$).

If there is a second dot, it follows exactly the same logic. What precedes the second dot, however, is the first dot. So the second dot is worth half the value of the first dot. Rather than dwell on this let's see it in practice. In the case of a double-dotted half note, the half note itself is worth two beats, the first dot is worth half of the note (one beat), and the second dot is worth half of the first dot (half a beat). Add those together and the double-dotted half note is worth 3½ beats (2+1+½). Again, it's simply a case of adding things together that are worth half of whatever preceded them.

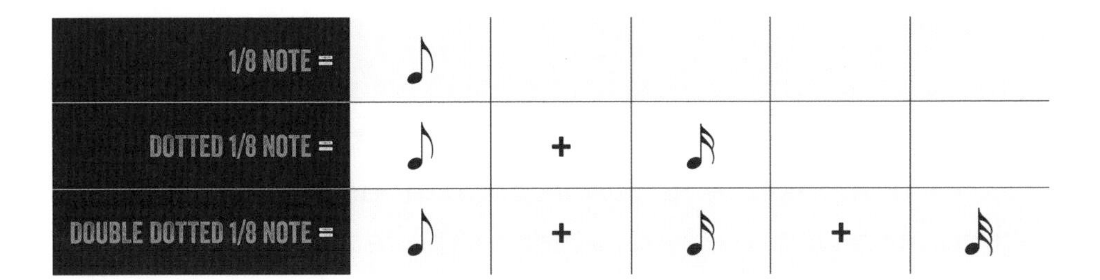

The notation below shows some typical rhythmic figures using double dots. The first half of the first bar shows a double-dotted eighth note beamed together with a 32nd note; this phrase is equivalent to one beat. The second beat shows the same two note values combined the opposite way around. In the second half of bar one, the 32nd notes have been replaced with 32nd-note rests. When organising bars with complex rhythms, for the sake of clarity, remember to avoid placing notes through the centre line.

The second bar shows how double dots can be applied to quarter notes. The quarter note itself is worth one beat, the first dot is worth half a beat, and the second dot is worth quarter of a beat. Notice again how those values are halving again each time. The total value of the double-dotted quarter note is 1¾ beats (1+½+¼).

In practice, it is usually better to avoid writing double dotted notes larger than a quarter note by splitting the rhythm down into smaller units and tying those notes together. This is simpler to read and can show the rhythmic structure in a clearer way. Double dots can also be applied to rests in the same way (as shown below), and should likewise be used conservatively for the very same reasons.

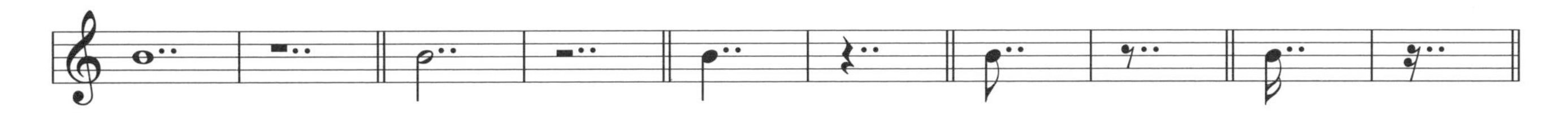

ODD NOTE GROUPINGS

The majority of the rhythms we have seen are based in 'simple' time, which means the beat is divisible by two. It is possible to divide the beat using odd numbers called tuplets. The most common is the triplet, which we have used previously to divide beats into three. Now we will use tuplets to divide beats into fives and sevens within a bar of 4/4. Odd note groupings are also known as 'irrational rhythms'.

QUINTUPLETS AND SEPTUPLETS

QUINTUPLETS ARE used to divide a beat into five equal notes. The simplest type of quintuplet to grasp is the 16th-note quintuplet, which squeezes five 16th notes into the space where there are usually four. Beats 1 and 2 of the first bar below show how 16th-note quintuplets are shown on the stave. You can get a feel for the sound of quintuplets by repeating the word 'hippopotamus' a few times without pausing for breath. The first two examples below shows quintuplets – five notes in the space where four notes would normally be placed. The septuplet examples below are similar in concept to the quintuplet examples, but this time the beats are divided into seven equal notes instead of five.

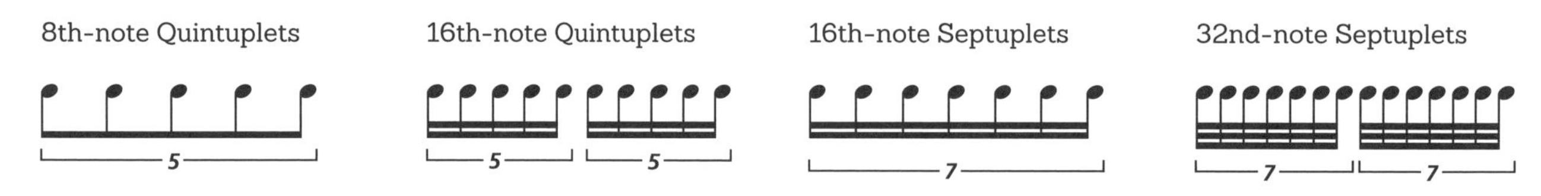

TUPLETS AS RATIOS

TUPLETS ARE usually written as a single number below a group of notes. If you see two sets of numbers, then a tuplet is being expressed as a ratio. The easiest way to understand what information is being given to you in the ratio is to think of it as 'X notes played in the space usually occupied by Y notes of this type'. For example, a group of eighth notes with a ratio of '3:2' means 'three eighth notes played in the space usually occupied by two eighth notes'. The notation below shows several tuplet groups expressed as ratios – try saying them aloud in the same way as the 3:2 ratio above.

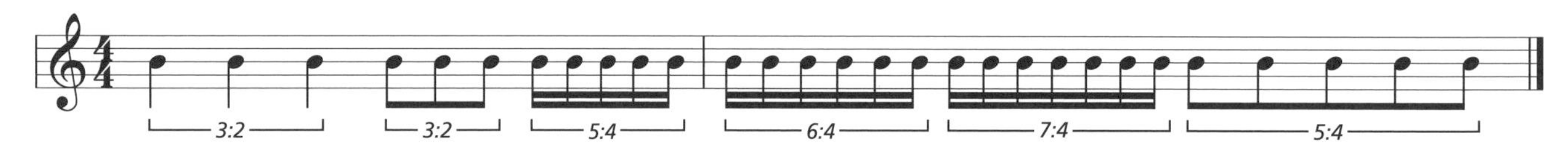

MORE TIME SIGNATURES

Much of Western popular music is written in 4/4 time, which was introduced in *Rockschool Popular Music Theory Guidebook 1*. 4/4, along with 3/4 and 2/4, is known as a 'simple' time signature because each beat is divisible by two. Guidebook 1 also introduced another category of time signature, in which the top numbers are a multiple of 3, called 'compound' time signatures – 12/8 and 6/8 are examples of compound time signatures used in popular music. *Guidebook 2* continues this exploration now by looking at some of the more unusual time signatures, such as 'odd' time signatures. 'Odd', in this instance, refers to 'uneven' as opposed to 'unusual', and as you will see from the artists and songs referenced, these time signatures have been a source or experimentation and inspiration to musicians of many genres for some considerable time.

ADVANCED METER

There are four pulses per bar in 4/4, and each pulse is equivalent to a quarter note in length. The length of a quarter note varies depending on the tempo, but if you are playing with a metronome, you can think of this as one note per click. If you use 4/4 as your baseline, you can understand odd times by comparing them with 4/4.

5/4 ODD

THE '4' in 5/4 means the pulse is a quarter note and therefore matches up with the click of a metronome. The number '5' at the top means there are five quarter-note pulses per bar. The easiest way to grasp this is to count '1 2 3 4 5' along to a metronome click. You can also try counting along with famous songs that use 5/4 such as Paul Desmond's 'Take 5' and Lalo Schifrin's 'Mission Impossible' theme. An easy way to get your head around 5/4 is to think of it as 4/4 with an extra quarter note.

6/4 COMPOUND DUPLE

6/4 IS essentially 4/4 with two extra quarter notes. Mathematically speaking, this is the same as two bars of 3/4 – although it doesn't sound the same. The time signature of a song is often defined by the placement of the snare drum, known as the backbeat. For a song in 3/4, such as Elliott Smith's 'Waltz #2', the snare typically falls on the second and third beat of each bar, so we hear '1 **2 3** 1 **2 3**'. In contrast, in 'Fell On Black Days' by Soundgarden the snare falls on the second, fourth and sixth beats, which is more like a 4/4 feel with an additional two beats, making '6/4' a more accurate description.

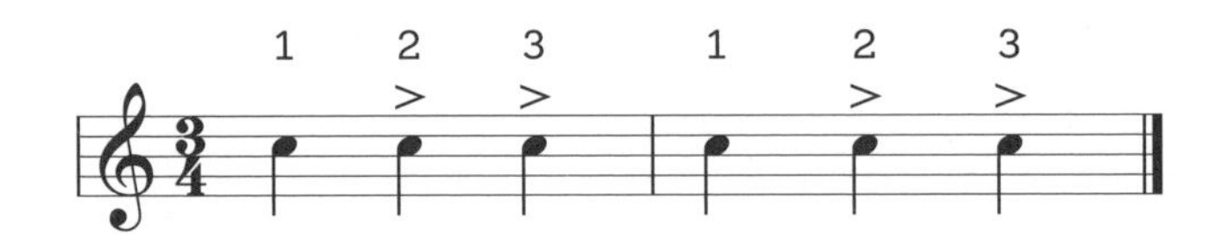

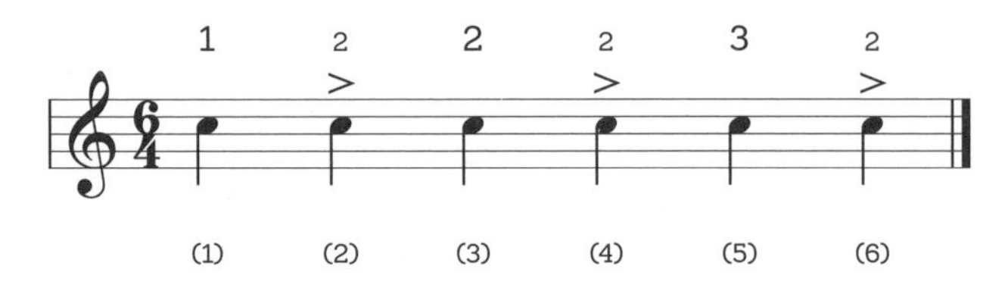

7/4 ODD

7/4 FOLLOWS the same logic as the previous two time signatures and is equal to seven quarter-note pulses (i.e. '1 2 3 4 5 6 7'). Sometimes it is easier to view 7/4 as a bar of 4/4 and a bar of 3/4 which have been glued together. Pink Floyd's 'Money' can be counted as alternating bars of 4/4 and 3/4, whereas Peter Gabriel's 'Solsbury Hill' feels like 3/4, then 4/4. Both songs would, however, be written as 7/4 to avoid having to write a new time signature at the beginning of each bar.

7/8 ODD

AN '8' shown at the bottom of a time signature means that the basic unit of measurement is an eighth note, rather than a quarter note as in the previous examples. 7/8 is one of the more natural-sounding odd times, as it feels like a truncated 4/4. You can hear a good example of it on the Rush song 'Subdivisions'. When we count eighth notes in common 4/4 time we count the downbeats and upbeats as follows: '1 & 2 & 3 & 4 &'. Removing the final eighth note provides the counting system for 7/8: '1 & 2 & 3 & 4'. Shown below are the common note groupings within bars of 7/8; the eighth notes can be beamed either as '4+3', or '3+4'.

5/8 ODD

5/8 IS one eighth-note shorter than a bar of 3/4, so can be counted '1 & 2 & 3'. 5/8 bars are relatively short and pass relatively quickly in songs like 'The Grudge' by Tool or 'Red' by King Crimson. This faster rate can make counting difficult, so grouping the count into groups of twos and threes is common. A bar of 5/8 can be grouped as 2+3, which can be verbalised as '1 2, 1 2 3'. It can also be phrased the other way around, 3+2, which would sound like '1 2 3, 1 2' (see notation below). This useful system not only works in 5/8 – every odd time signature can be broken down into groups of twos and threes.

2/2 AND 3/2 CUT COMMON AND SIMPLE TRIPLE

SOMETIMES THE half note is used as the basic unit of measurement; this is shown with the number '2' as the lower note in the time signature. 2/2 is also known as 'cut time' and means that there are two half notes per bar. This is mathematically the same length as a bar of 4/4, but instead of tapping your foot four times per bar, you tap it only twice. This gives a different feel, which is more suited to faster-tempo music such as bluegrass, samba or military marches.

THE METHODS we use to count and feel time signatures can be highly personal, but there are some long standing conventions that have been used historically. With regards to 2/2 and 3/2 the teaching has long been to count the half note/minim pulse as denoted above the stave in the examples below. Alternatively, some contemporary music may well lend itself to the method written beneath the stave.

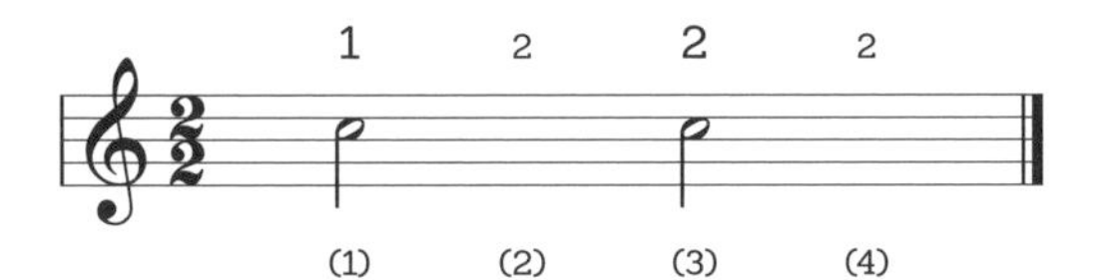

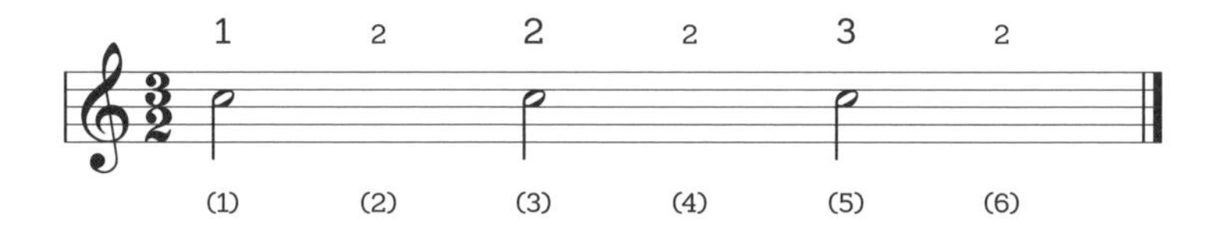

MODES

The distinction between 'major' or 'minor' gives only a relatively broad description of scales. Those names only really tell you that the scale either has a major 3rd or a minor 3rd, but there are many variations of major and minor scales. These variations are called modes, and each one has a unique flavour because it contains a unique set of intervals. Remembering lots of different intervals can be confusing, so in this chapter we will compare the modes to scales you already know, reducing the amount of new information you need to memorise.

MODES

ONE SCALE, SEVEN MODES

IF YOU are already acquainted with the concept of relative major and minor scales, then the idea of using the same notes to create different sounds will be a familiar one. To make sure, let's briefly recap the theory of 'major and minor relativity'.

The C major scale has seven notes, CDEFGABC, with the note spacing T T S T T T S, which translates as the following intervals: 1 2 3 4 5 6 7. C major's relative minor is A minor, which contains the notes ABCDEFGA. These are the same notes as the C major scale, but the starting note (A) and note spacing (T S T T S T T) are different. This time the intervals are 1 2 ♭3 4 5 ♭6 ♭7.

To sum up, different note spacing means different intervals, and different intervals create different scales, or – as we'll discuss in this chapter – modes.

The relative minor always starts from the 6th note of the major scale, but we can also start the scale from the 2nd, 3rd, 4th, 5th and 7th notes to produce other scales. For example, let's start the C major scale from each note of the scale, one by one.

MODE / SPACING		T		T		S		T		T		T		S		T		T		S		T		T		T	
C IONIAN	C		D		E		F		G		A		B		C												
D DORIAN			D		E		F		G		A		B		C		D										
E PHRYGIAN					E		F		G		A		B		C		D		E								
F LYDIAN							F		G		A		B		C		D		E		F						
G MIXOLYDIAN									G		A		B		C		D		E		F		G				
A AEOLIAN											A		B		C		D		E		F		G		A		
B LOCRIAN													B		C		D		E		F		G		A		B

The 'new scales' are shown from top to bottom in the table on page 16, and the note spacing is shown from left to right. The irregular tone and semitone gaps between the notes (shown in red) are key to giving each mode its unique structure.

Each unique note spacing translates to a particular set of intervals and, consequently, leads to seven different modes: Ionian, Dorian, Phrygian, Lydian, Mixolydian, Aeolian and Locrian. The names 'Ionian' and 'Aeolian' are the Greek modal names for the major and minor scales, respectively, so you are actually already familiar with those two modes.

The seven modes correspond to each of the seven chords of the harmonised major scale, and the chord is a clue as to the general sound of the scale. This chord-scale relationship is the same in every key, so it will always be the same (see table below). For example, the Dorian mode always goes with a minor 7 chord.

MODE	CHORD	INTERVALS
IONIAN (MAJOR)	MAJOR 7	1 2 3 4 5 6 7
DORIAN	MINOR 7	1 2 ♭3 4 5 6 ♭7
PHRYGIAN	MINOR 7	1 ♭2 ♭3 4 5 ♭6 ♭7
LYDIAN	MAJOR 7	1 2 3 ♯4 5 6 7
MIXOLYDIAN	DOMINANT 7	1 2 3 4 5 6 ♭7
AEOLIAN (NATURAL MINOR)	MINOR 7	1 2 ♭3 4 5 ♭6 ♭7
LOCRIAN	MINOR 7♭5	1 ♭2 ♭3 4 ♭5 ♭6 ♭7

Now let's reorganise the modes and group them into similar chord sounds. This will help you to memorise the intervals and appreciate the practical application of each mode. As the table below shows, the modes can be grouped into three categories: major, minor and half diminished.

MAJOR MODES	MINOR MODES	HALF DIMINISHED
IONIAN	AEOLIAN	LOCRIAN
LYDIAN	DORIAN	
MIXOLYDIAN	PHRYGIAN	

MAJOR MODES

THE THREE major modes are Ionian, Lydian and Mixolydian. These are the first, fourth and fifth modes of the major scale. These modes are seen as major because they all contain a major 3rd, but they have much more in common than that. All three contain a major pentatonic scale inside them. The major pentatonic intervals are 1 2 3 5 6; to complete the seven-note mode, we need to add a 4th and a 7th interval.

A 4th interval can be either a perfect 4th or an augmented 4th. Similarly, a 7th interval can be a major 7th or a minor 7th. You can add any combination of these different 4ths and 7ths to the major pentatonic to create different-sounding modes. We will look at the three major modes all from the same root note, C, because this way the similarities and, more importantly, the differences between them will become apparent.

The table below shows the major pentatonic intervals across the top and the different combinations of 4th and 7th intervals which are required to complete each desired mode. Using this approach, you only need to remember the specific 4ths and 7ths for each mode.

MAJOR PENTATONIC	1	2	3	—	5	6	—
IONIAN				4			7
LYDIAN				♯4			7
MIXOLYDIAN				4			♭7

IONIAN

THE IONIAN mode is another name for the major scale and corresponds to the I chord of the harmonised major scale. The Ionian has an innocent, happy sound, which has been used in pop music through the ages, but perhaps one of the most iconic Ionian song is Rodgers and Hammerstein's 'Do-Re-Mi' song from *The Sound Of Music*. The C Ionian contains the notes C D E F G A B and is shown below on the stave.

LYDIAN

THE LYDIAN is the fourth mode of the major scale. It has a sweet, uplifting sound due to its unique combination of intervals: 1 2 3 ♯4 5 6 7. As you can see, the intervallic structure is very similar to the Ionian mode's, except the fourth note is raised by a semitone. This ♯4th is the main characteristic of the mode, as the Lydian is the only mode to contain this interval. The Lydian sound is used extensively by film and TV composers like John Williams, Alan Silvestri and Danny Elfman to evoke a sense of magic and playfulness, particularly in their scores for *E.T.*, *Back To The Future* and most famously, the theme from *The Simpsons*. The notes of C Lydian are C D E F♯ G A B and appear on the stave like this.

MIXOLYDIAN

THE MIXOLYDIAN is the fifth mode of the major scale and has a similar intervallic structure to its parent: 1 2 3 4 5 6 ♭7. As you can see, the intervals of the Mixolydian are almost exactly the same as those of the major scale, except for the 7th degree. The Mixolydian is the only major mode to contain a ♭7th, which makes it the obvious choice for playing over dominant 7 chords. The Mixolydian contains all five notes of the major pentatonic (just like the other major modes), which gives it a light and bright character, but the addition of the 4th and ♭7th intervals suggest a hint of minor pentatonic. This hint makes the Mixolydian a popular mode in blues, funk and soul – genres that often depend on this major/minor ambiguity. The notes of C Mixolydian are C D E F G A B♭, which appear on the stave as follows.

MINOR MODES

THE THREE minor modes – Aeolian, Dorian and Phrygian – are the sixth, second and third modes of the major scale, and correspond to the three minor chords in the harmonised major scale. These modes are seen as minor because they all contain a minor 3rd; additionally, they all contain the notes of the minor pentatonic scale. The minor pentatonic intervals are 1 ♭3 4 5 ♭7, so to complete each of the seven-note minor modes, you need to add a 2nd and a 6th interval.

A 2nd interval can be either a minor 2nd or a major 2nd. Similarly, a 6th interval can be a major 6th or a minor 6th. You can add any combination of these different 2nds and 6ths to the minor pentatonic to create different-sounding modes. We will look at the three minor modes all from the same root note, A, so that the similarities and differences between them will be more obvious.

The table below shows the minor pentatonic intervals across the top and the different combinations of 2nd and 6th intervals which complete each mode. Using this approach, you only need to remember the 2nds and 6ths for each mode.

MINOR PENTATONIC	1	—	♭3	4	5	—	♭7
AEOLIAN		2				♭6	
DORIAN		2				6	
PHRYGIAN		♭2				♭6	

AEOLIAN

THE AEOLIAN mode is another name for the natural minor scale. It is the sixth mode of the major scale. To complete this mode, you start with the minor pentatonic intervals, then add a major 2nd and a minor 6th. In the key of A minor, the Aeolian mode has the notes A B C D E F G. This mode has a sad sound, which is often used in songs that have loss as their subject matter, such as REM's 'Losing My Religion' and Adele's 'Someone Like You'.

DORIAN

DORIAN IS the second mode of the major scale and corresponds with the IIm chord, which can be a minor triad or a minor 7 chord. If you start with the A minor pentatonic scale (A_CDE_G), you can turn it into A Dorian by filling in the gaps. The extra intervals needed are the major 2nd (B) and major 6th (F♯). The Dorian is the only minor mode with a major 6th, which provides one of its main characteristics, adding a cool brightness to the otherwise minor tonality. Pink Floyd's 'Another Brick In The Wall (Part 2)' is a classic Dorian song. The A Dorian mode contains the notes A B C D E F♯ G and is shown on the stave below.

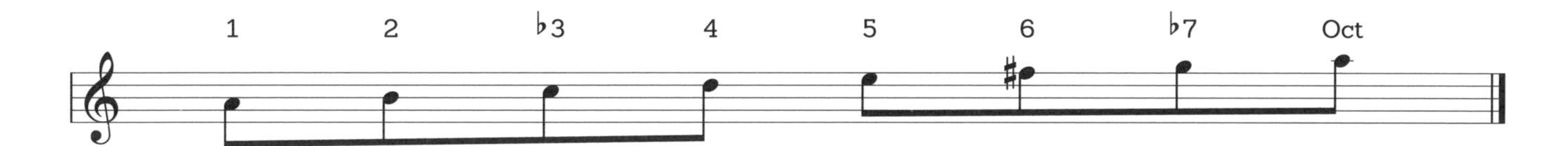

PHRYGIAN

THE PHRYGIAN mode is the third mode of the major scale and matches up with the IIIm chord, which could be a minor triad or a minor 7 chord. If you use the minor pentatonic intervals (1 ♭3 4 5 ♭7) as a starting point, the two additional Phrygian intervals are a ♭2nd and a ♭6th. This is the only one of the three minor modes that has a ♭2nd interval, which gives it a distinctive sound. The ♭2nd has a dark and foreboding quality, used to great effect by John Williams in his theme for the film *Jaws*. This quality makes the Phrygian a popular choice in rock and metal. The A Phrygian mode contains the notes A B♭ C D E F G and is shown on the stave below.

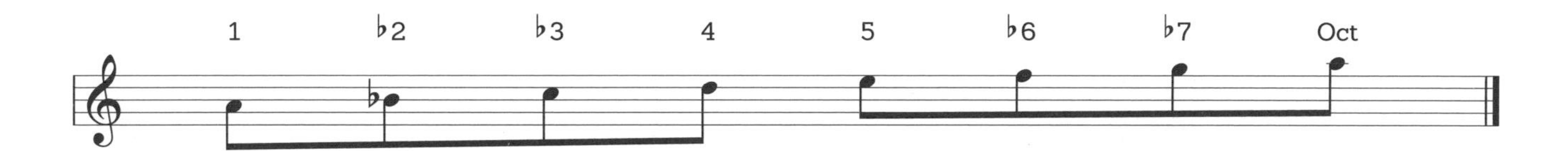

LOCRIAN

THE LOCRIAN is the seventh mode of the major scale and corresponds to the min7♭5 chord. Although the scale has a minor 3rd, it is not included with the minor modes because its ♭5 puts it in the diminished category. The Locrian is the darkest and most ominous sounding of all the modes because every interval is flattened, with the exception of the 4th. Due to its tense sound, the Locrian is rarely heard for an extended period. It is sometimes used in jazz, played over the min7♭5 or 'half-diminished' (ø) chords in standards such as Kenny Dorham's 'Blue Bossa' and Cole Porter's 'Night And Day'. However, these instances are no longer than a single bar in length.

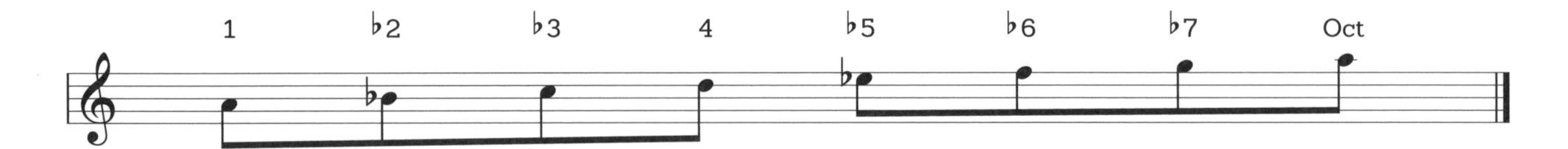

LIGHT TO DARK

IN THE table below we have organised the modes in terms of the mood they convey: Lydian being the brightest and Locrian the darkest. Perhaps not coincidentally, this also places the modes with the most similar intervals next to one another. Starting with Lydian and moving down the list, you can get from one mode to the next only by flattening one note at a time: flatten the ♯4th to a perfect 4th and you get Ionian; flatten the major 7th of Ionian to a ♭7th and you have Mixolydian. As you continue to flatten intervals one by one, you will get: Dorian, Aeolian, Phrygian and finally Locrian, which has five flattened intervals. The pairs of 'squared' notes on the diagram indicate the notes which change from mode to mode.

MODE	INTERVALS						
LYDIAN	1	2	3	♯4	5	6	7
IONIAN	1	2	3	4	5	6	7
MIXOLYDIAN	1	2	3	4	5	6	♭7
DORIAN	1	2	♭3	4	5	6	♭7
AEOLIAN	1	2	♭3	4	5	♭6	♭7
PHRYGIAN	1	♭2	♭3	4	5	♭6	♭7
LOCRIAN	1	♭2	♭3	4	♭5	♭6	♭7

MODAL KEY SIGNATURES

THERE ARE two schools of thought on using key signatures to write modal music. The problem is there are key signatures for every major and minor key, but no symbol for D Dorian or D Lydian, for example. The common solution is to use the major or minor key signature that most closely matches the mode in question. In this case, D Dorian would be written in the key of D minor and D Lydian in the key of D major. The notes that do not fit the key are then adjusted using accidentals (see below). The advantage of this system is that the key signature shows the tonal centre and the accidentals highlight those special intervals that make the mode different from the parent key.

The second approach is the modal key signature, where you use the parent key that the mode comes from. We started this chapter with a table showing the C major scale and its seven derivative modes. Using the modal key signature method, all of the modes of C major would use the same key signature, i.e. no sharps or flats.

To calculate the modal key signature, first you must determine the numerical position of the mode in the sequence shown in the table below. This sequence is the same for every key. If, for example, you are playing G Mixolydian, the parent scale's root note is found either a perfect 5th down or a perfect 4th up – either way, you will arrive at the key of C. The table shows each mode and its intervallic relationship to the root note. Both ascending and descending intervals are shown, so you are free to choose the shortest or longest distance to the destination note.

MODE	DISTANCE TO PARENT KEY (ASCENDING INTERVAL)	DISTANCE TO PARENT KEY (DESCENDING INTERVAL)
IONIAN	HAS THE SAME ROOT NOTE	HAS THE SAME ROOT NOTE
DORIAN	UP A MINOR 7TH	DOWN A MAJOR 2ND
PHRYGIAN	UP A MINOR 6TH	DOWN A MAJOR 3RD
LYDIAN	UP A PERFECT 5TH	DOWN A PERFECT 4TH
MIXOLYDIAN	UP A PERFECT 4TH	DOWN A PERFECT 5TH
AEOLIAN	UP A MINOR 3RD	DOWN A MAJOR 6TH
LOCRIAN	UP A MINOR 2ND	DOWN A MAJOR 7TH

MODAL CHORD PROGRESSIONS

The key of C contains the following seven triads: C major, D minor, E minor, F major, G major, A minor and B diminished. These can also be played as 7th chords: C major 7, D minor 7, E minor 7, F major 7, G dominant 7, A minor 7, B minor 7♭5. If you play these chords starting on C, this immediately establishes that the C chord is the tonal centre (or home) to which your ear expects the progression to return.

Using modal progressions, it is possible to make any one of the chords the tonal centre and create the sound of Dorian, Phrygian, Lydian etc. The idea is to arrange the chords in such a way that your ear doesn't expect the progression to return to C major.

In the table below, notice how each mode uses the same chords, but these chords are offset by one each time you move from one mode to the next.

MODE	1	2	3	4	5	6	7
IONIAN	Cmaj7	Dm7	Em7	Fmaj7	G7	Am7	Bm7♭5
DORIAN	Dm7	Em7	Fmaj7	G7	Am7	Bm7♭5	Cmaj7
PHRYGIAN	Em7	Fmaj7	G7	Am7	Bm7♭5	Cmaj7	Dm7
LYDIAN	Fmaj7	G7	Am7	Bm7♭5	Cmaj7	Dm7	Em7
MIXOLYDIAN	G7	Am7	Bm7♭5	Cmaj7	Dm7	Em7	Fmaj7
AEOLIAN	Am7	Bm7♭5	Cmaj7	Dm7	Em7	Fmaj7	G7
LOCRIAN	Bm7♭5	Cmaj7	Dm7	Em7	Fmaj7	G7	Am7

When making modal chord progressions it is a good idea to start with the first chord in the mode's harmonised sequence. For example, D Dorian would start with the

D minor chord, F Lydian would start with an F major 7, and so on. You must also take into account the tone and semitone spacing between the related chords, as this structure is what gives each mode its identity. For example, a minor chord could be the first chord of the Dorian, Aeolian or Phrygian modes, but placing a major chord a semitone above the minor chord makes the sequence uniquely Phrygian.

This table summarises the Roman numerals, triads and 7th chords for each step of the key of C major as well as the tone/semitone spacing for each chord, and, finally, the position of each modal key centre.

I		II		III		IV		V		VI		VII		I
C	T	D	T	E	S	F	T	G	T	A	T	B	S	C
maj		min		min		maj		maj		min		dim		maj
maj7		m7		m7		maj7		7		m7		m7♭5		maj7
IONIAN		DORIAN		PHRYGIAN		LYDIAN		MIXOLYDIAN		AEOLIAN		LOCRIAN		IONIAN

Here are some simple progressions that typify each derivative mode of the C major parent key.

MODE TONIC	CHORD PROGRESSION	ROMAN NUMERALS
C IONIAN	C – G(7) – F	I – V(7) – IV
D DORIAN	Dm – Em	IIm – IIIm
E PHRYGIAN	Em – F	IIIm – IV
F LYDIAN	F – G(7)	IV – V(7)
G MIXOLYDIAN	G – F – C	V – IV – I
A AEOLIAN	Am – Dm – Em	VIm – IIm – IIIm
B LOCRIAN	Bm7♭5 – F	VIIm7♭5 – IV

CONTINUED

MODAL PROGRESSIONS CONTINUED...

NOW WE will look at each modal progression in more depth. Notice that we have written each mode on the stave below using the modal key signature method, with C major as the parent key.

C IONIAN I V IV

C IS the natural tonal centre for these chords to return to. The primary triads I IV V have served blues, pop and rock songwriters for decades, and the I V IV progression, specifically, is the basis of The Who's 'Baba O'Riley'.

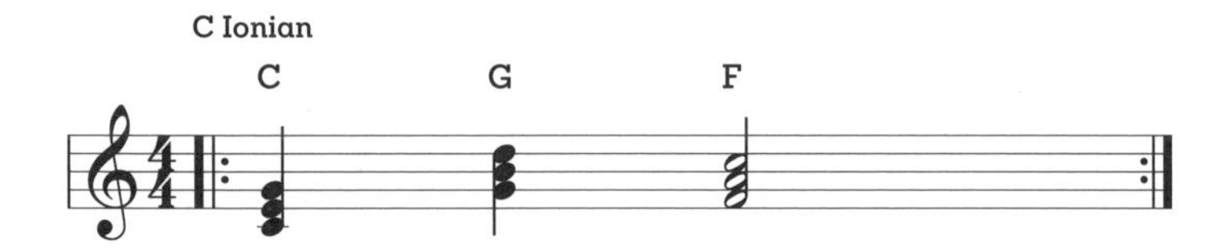

D DORIAN IIm IIIm

TWO MINOR 7 chords played a tone apart can only be the IIm and IIIm chords. The IIm chord has the intervals 1 ♭3 5 ♭7, and the IIIm chord adds the intervals, 2, 4 and 6. These are all the intervals of the Dorian mode.

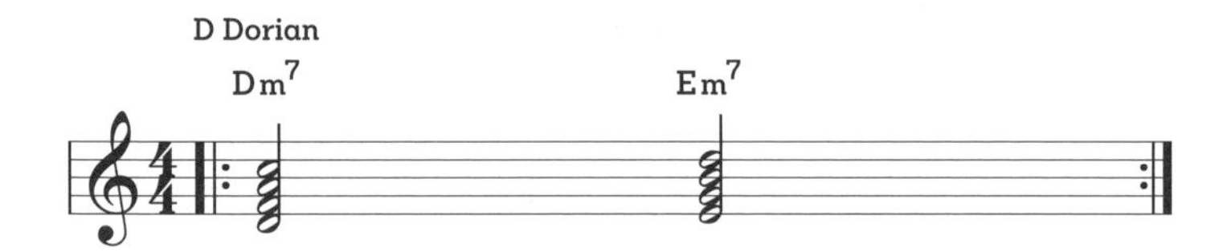

E PHRYGIAN IIIm IV

THIS PROGRESSION uses the IIIm and IV chords – this is the only place where a minor chord and a major chord are a semitone apart. If you start with an E minor chord, this immediately establishes the tonal centre for the listener. Follow the E minor with an F major, and the ♭2 bass movement is unmistakably Phrygian.

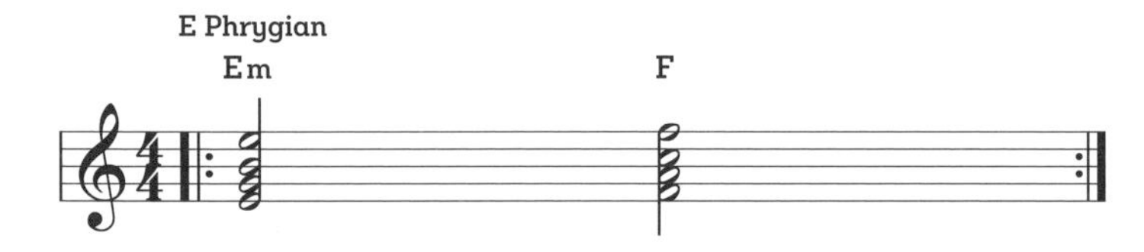

F LYDIAN IV V

THE LYDIAN mode starts on the IV chord, which is accompanied nicely by the V chord a tone above. These are the only two major chords a tone apart, so this is uniquely Lydian. The sound of the IV chord extended to a major 7♯11 is quintessentially Lydian.

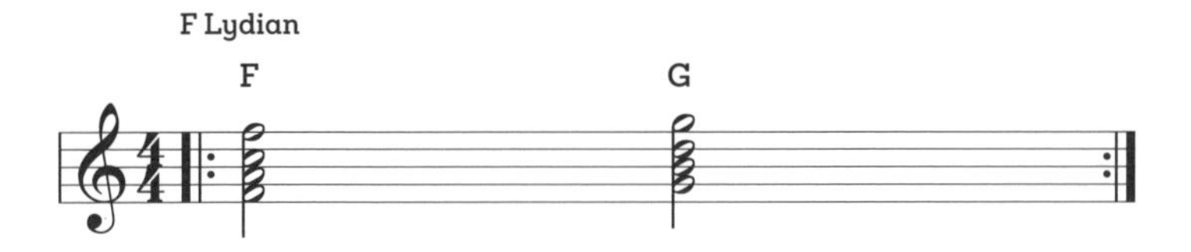

G MIXOLYDIAN V IV I

THE V IV I triads provide the Mixolydian sound featured famously on Lynyrd Skynyrd's 'Sweet Home Alabama'. To highlight the importance of emphasis in the human ear's perception of modes, notice that this is essentially the same progression as the Ionian I V IV, but we hear it differently depending on what chord is played first.

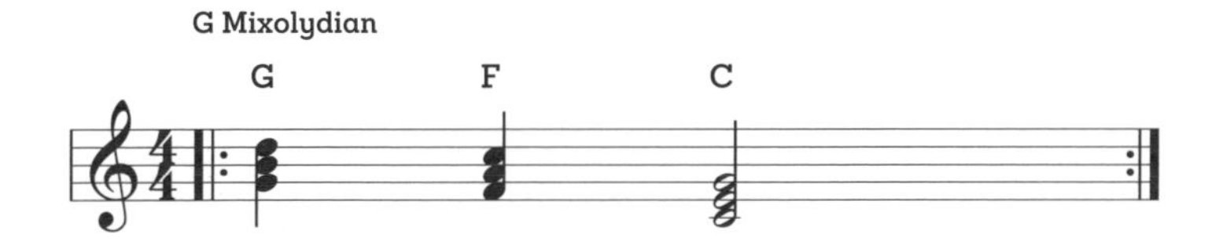

A AEOLIAN VIm IIm IIIm

THE THREE minor triads of the key are the VIm IIm and IIIm, which effectively form a minor Im IVm Vm progression starting from the sixth degree of the major scale.

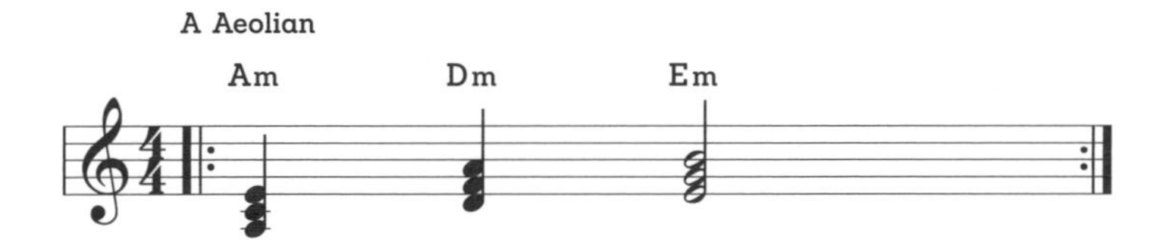

B LOCRIAN VIIm7♭5 IV

LOCRIAN PROGRESSIONS sound inherently strange and unresolved, as illustrated by these two chords placed a tritone apart. For this reason, this is a seldom-used mode.

ADVANCED SCALES

Along with being tested on your scale knowledge in the Popular Music Harmony section of Rockschool Theory Exams at Grades 6–8, a good understanding of scales and how they can relate to musical style is something that will hold you in good stead in the Band Analysis section of an exam. Grades 6–8 add four new musical styles to the pool from which the examination scores can be drawn – jazz, country, soul and reggae. One of these styles in particular, jazz, is notable for its use of a more sophisticated musical vocabulary, and this chapter introduces several scales that feature heavily in jazz, along with one that is synonymous with country music.

SYMMETRICAL SCALES

The first three scales we'll be looking at are known as symmetrical scales because their scale formulas form repetitive patterns. On the piano keyboard some of these scales even produce clusters of notes that look like mirror-imaged patterns of themselves, such as in the case of the whole-tone and diminished scales. They're not as uncommon as you might assume when listening to them for the first time, and while they're not exactly commonplace, they are frequently heard in particular genres such as jazz and progressive metal.

THE CHROMATIC SCALE

MUCH LIKE Bigfoot, the chromatic scale is something that is often seen in fleeting glimpses in the wild, rather than in full. The term 'chromatic' comes from the Greek word for colour, 'chroma' – the inference being that it contains 'all the colours'. It is created from a series of semitones (S S S S S S S S S S S S) and so encompasses every single available note between two points. In written form, chromatic scales are best written out with sharps when ascending and flats when descending, as this cuts down on the number of accidentals required in the notation:

While full-blown examples of chromatic scales are thin on the ground in popular music, short chromatic fragments can be heard in almost every genre. In rock, for example, you can hear descending chromatic passages in the verse riff of Led Zeppelin's 'Dazed And Confused'.

WHOLE-TONE SCALE

THE WHOLE-TONE scale is a symmetrical scale with the formula T T T T T T. While remembering the formula is far from challenging, finding somewhere to play it (without being fired from the band) is quite another matter. Before going any further, listen to the first two tracks highlighted in the *Hear It Here* boxout below. Both tracks use the whole-tone scale in the first few seconds of the intro as a kind of 'special effect' scale, drawing on its exotic, other-worldly character.

Because of the symmetrical nature, there are only two whole-tone scales, although as it's not a conventional seven-note construction, there are numerous ways to spell it.

C WHOLE-TONE SCALE	C	D	E	F♯	G♯	A♯	C
D♭ WHOLE-TONE SCALE	D♭	E♭	F	G	A	B	D♭

Another place that the scale sees some action is in jazz, as one of the options for playing over altered dominant chords such as C7♭5 and C7♯5. Here the whole-tone scale acts as a curious type of dominant scale where the intervals are laid out as follows:

C WHOLE-TONE SCALE	C	D	E	G♭	G♯	B♭	C
INTERVALS	1	2	3	♭5	♯5	♭7	1

DIMINISHED SCALE – HALF/WHOLE

THE DIMINISHED scale comes in two varieties – [1] the half/whole and [2] the whole/half. They sound very similar but care has to be taken to use them in the right place. The terms 'half/whole' and 'whole/half' refer to the arrangement of tones (whole) and semitones (half) in the scale formula, in this case 'S T S T S T S T':

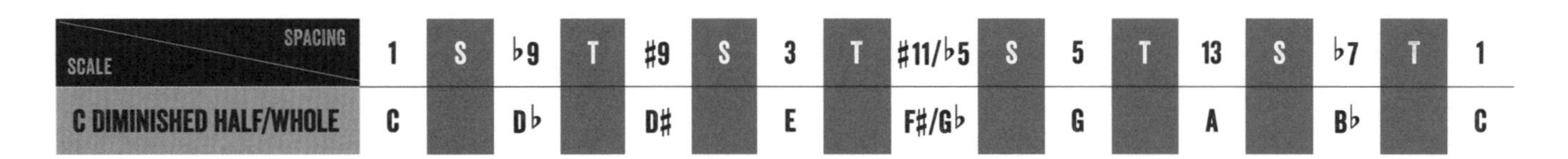

SCALE / SPACING	1	S	♭9	T	♯9	S	3	T	♯11/♭5	S	5	T	13	S	♭7	T	1
C DIMINISHED HALF/WHOLE	C		D♭		D♯		E		F♯/G♭		G		A		B♭		C

As you can see, the pattern of semi-tone/tone is constantly repeated. Whenever we see a repeated pattern of intervals throughout an entire scale, the scale is referred to as 'symmetrical'. In this instance, the scale formula gives us the intervals: 1, ♭2, ♯2, 3, ♯4/♭5, 5, 6, ♭7. Although referred to as a diminished scale, the half/whole scale is often used over dominant chords. Some of you may have noticed that this is the first scale we have introduced that contains 8 different notes.

As with many of the scales in this section of the book, the diminished scale sees much of its use in jazz, where it's often employed over dominant 7th chords such as 7♭9, 7♭9♯11, 13♭9♯11. It's extremely versatile because it contains all of the following intervals: 3, ♭5/♯11, 5, 13, ♭7, ♭9, ♯9.

DIMINISHED SCALE – WHOLE/HALF

THE WHOLE/HALF version of the diminished scale has the formula 'T S T S T S T S'. As you can see, simply by starting on the second degree of this scale you will end up playing the half/whole instead of the whole/half – the scales are in effect modes of one another. The whole-half diminished scale is the predominant scale of choice to play, sing, or compose over diminished chords, whereas the half-whole diminished scale is used predominantly over dominant chords.

SCALE / SPACING	1	T	9	S	♭3	T	11	S	♭5	T	♭13	S	♭♭7	T	7	S	1
C DIMINISHED WHOLE/HALF	C		D		E♭		F		G♭		A♭		B♭♭		B		C

COUNTRY SCALE

Popular Music Theory Guidebook 1 introduced the minor pentatonic scale and how it has an 'almost identical twin', the blues scale. The only difference between the scales is an extra note in the blues scale – the ♭5 interval often referred to as the 'blue note'. It also introduced the major pentatonic scale (the relative major of the minor pentatonic scale). This scale also has a close relative – the 'country' scale, which also has an extra note appearing (relatively speaking!) in exactly the same position within the scale as the blue note. The following table shows how the different scales are related:

A MINOR PENTATONIC	A	C	D		E	G	A	
A BLUES	A	C	D	E♭	E	G	A	
C MAJOR PENTATONIC		C	D		E	G	A	C
C COUNTRY		C	D	E♭	E	G	A	C

The country scale sounds best played over straight diatonic major key chord progressions. While the blue note acted as a ♭5th in the blues scale, the 'extra note' in the country scale translates into a ♭3rd. It's important to note that in both cases this note generally acts as a chromatic passing note between the notes it sits between. However, skilled soloists in the respective genres often play on the difference between these pitches to create tensions and resolutions in their solos.

MELODIC MINOR SCALE

On first listen, there's nothing readily apparent about the melodic minor scale to hint at the vast wealth of resources it contains. Like the major scale, a series of modes can be created from the melodic minor scale, and these are the source of many of the distinctive sounds of contemporary jazz improvisation. In Grades 6–8 of Rockschool's Popular Music Theory exams, you need to know two of these: the melodic minor scale itself and its seventh mode, the altered scale.

THE MELODIC MINOR SCALE

ONE WAY to view the melodic minor scale is to compare it to a natural minor scale – by raising the 6th and 7th degrees of the natural minor scale by a semitone you arrive at the melodic minor scale. As the A natural minor scale contains no sharps or flats, the accidentals in the following notation serve to highlight the difference between the natural minor scale and the melodic minor scale:

If you're from a classical music background you'll notice that there's no mention of a descending version of the scale – in popular music theory there is no such distinction.

The melodic minor is often used in jazz over vamps centred around chord Im, and you can hear this on Wes Montgomery's 'S.O.S.' from the album *Full House*. It's often used in the melodies of other genres over functional and secondary-dominant chords in minor keys, such as the "all my troubles" phrase in The Beatles' song 'Yesterday' from the album *Help!* (1965).

THE ALTERED SCALE

YOU WILL already have encountered the term 'altered' in relation to chords, where it implies a dominant chord in which the 5ths and 9ths are those from the altered scale, such as C7♯5♭9. The altered scale is named as it is because many of these same intervals are altered in the same way, although you may also hear it referred to as the 'superlocrian'. Let's look at the scale written out in the simplest possible way:

So the altered scale is 1 ♭2 ♭3 ♭4 ♭5 ♭6 ♭7 is it? This looks pretty straightforward, but it's not telling us anything particularly useful about how the altered scale works against altered chords. In the following example the intervals of the scale have been written out to show why the scale is so useful for using over altered chords:

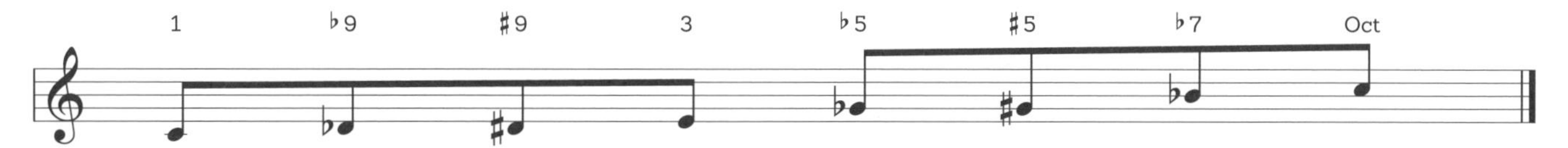

This really gets to the heart of the scale – it has a major 3rd and a flattened 7th, which should immediately make you think of dominant 7 chords. It also has both a ♭5 and a ♯5, and also a ♭9 and a ♯9. Now you can see why it is often used in jazz (and occasionally blues) over chords such as 7♭5, 7♯5, 7♭9, 7♯9, 7♯5♭9 and 7♯5♯9.

The altered scale is a great introduction to the modes of the melodic minor scale, which often feature as a core area of study in Diploma- and Degree-level courses in popular music, and are an absolute must if you choose to specialise in jazz.

rockschool®

TRANSPOSITION

Transposition means moving a melody, scale, chord or chord progression from its original pitch to a different pitch, higher or lower. A simple melody such as 'Happy Birthday' can be played starting from any one of 12 different root notes in a variety of different octaves. In this chapter we will use the C major scale as a constant and apply all manner of transposing techniques to it. The scale is used only as an illustration; remember that the same processes can be applied to any melody or chord progression in any key.

TRANSPOSING WITHOUT A KEY SIGNATURE

Every major scale has the same note spacing: 'Tone Tone Semitone Tone Tone Tone Semitone'. C major is the only key with no sharp or flats, so transposing a C major scale or melody to a different key means adding sharps or flats, also known as accidentals. Depending on the key, this could mean adding anything from one to seven accidentals. The reason for this is to move notes up or down a semitone so the spaces between the notes are consistent with the major scale pattern, 'T T S T T T S'.

TRANSPOSING UP A PERFECT 5TH (G MAJOR SCALE)

THE FIRST step in transposing a C major scale or melody up a perfect 5th to G major is to draw the notes G, A, B, C, D, E, F and G as dots on the relevant lines and spaces of the stave. When moving from a line to a space or a space to a line, the interval travelled is a tone – except for B to C and E to F, which are intervals of a semitone. This has to be taken into account and corrected. On the first bar below you can see that the spacing of all the notes is consistent with the major scale except the last two spaces. In the second bar this has been corrected by raising the F to F♯.

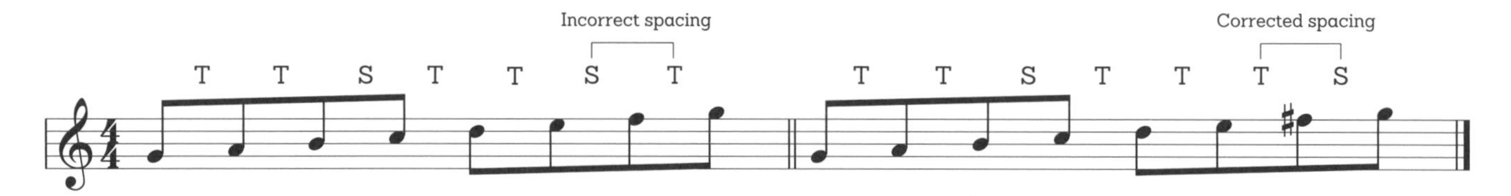

TRANSPOSING UP A PERFECT 4TH (F MAJOR SCALE)

TO TRANSPOSE C major up a perfect 4th to F major, once again draw the notes on the stave (this time, F, G, A, B, C, D, E and F), then check the interval spacing is consistent with the major scale. Below you can see that the spaces between the notes A, B and C are incorrect in the first bar, but have been corrected in the second bar by lowering the B to B♭.

TRANSPOSING WITH A KEY SIGNATURE

Accidentals are useful if a piece of music changes key temporarily for a bar or two. If the piece remains in a new key for a considerable amount of time, then it is better to place a key signature at the beginning of the section. This means that the sharps and flats indicated in the key signature will prevail for the rest of the piece, or until a new key signature is introduced.

SHARP KEYS (CIRCLE OF 5THS)

ADDING SHARPS one by one automatically transposes the key up in 5ths, a system known as the circle of 5ths. The sharp notes are added in the following order: F♯ C♯ G♯ D♯ A♯ E♯ B♯. A useful mnemonic for memorising this is 'Father Charles Goes Down And Ends Battle'. The sharps are added from left to right and always appear in the same formation, which you can think of as 'up, down, up, down, down, up, down'. You can quickly recognise the sharp keys by looking at the sharp symbol farthest to the right then going up a semitone; the note you arrive at is the key.

FLAT KEYS (CYCLE OF 4THS)

ADDING FLATS one by one automatically transposes the key up in 4ths, a system known as the cycle of 4ths. The flat notes are also added in the opposite order as the sharp notes (B♭ E♭ A♭ D♭ G♭ C♭ F♭) and, helpfully, the mnemonic works backwards, too: 'Battle Ends And Down Goes Charles' Father'. The flats are added from left to right and always appear in the same formation, which is 'down, up, down, up, down, up, down'.

On the bass clef, both the sharps and flats appear in exactly the same formations, only moved down one line or space to match up with the notes of that clef.

TRANSPOSING UP A PERFECT 5TH

Transposing the C major scale up a perfect 5th requires a sequence of four steps. The fifth note of the current scale will be the root note of the destination key, so first count up five notes: 'C D E F **G**'. Now you know the new key is G and you can use the circle of 5ths to work out how many sharps to add. The circle of 5ths is C **G** D A E B F♯ C♯ and the respective number of sharps for each key is 0 **1** 2 3 4 5 6 7, so the key of G contains one sharp. Now, refer to the 'Father Charles' mnemonic to work out that the first sharpened note is F. Finally, shift all the notes up two lines or two spaces.

TRANSPOSING UP A MAJOR 3RD

To transpose up a major 3rd, start by counting up three notes, 'C D **E**', to work out the starting point for the destination key. Next, count through the circle of 5ths until you arrive at E: 'C G D A **E**'. E is the 5th key in the circle, and therefore has four sharps. Those four sharps are added to the beginning of the stave in the order 'F C G D' from left to right. Finally, shift the notes up a major 3rd, which is equivalent to moving up one line or one space.

In short, those four steps are:

1 Count through the original scale to determine the destination key.

2 Refer to the circle of 5ths/cycle of 4ths to find the number of sharps or flats.

3 Identify sharps and flats using a mnemonic; add to the stave from left to right.

4 Shift all the notes up the same distance.

THE 'CYCLE' OF FOURTHS AND THE 'CIRCLE' OF FIFTHS

YOU MAY have noticed the difference in terminology between the 'cycle' of 4ths and 'circle' of 5ths. This is another convention of nomenclature which definitely justifies definition.

The 'cycle' of 4ths is so-called as the term actually refers to the fact that chords resolve predominantly around the 'cycle' of perfect 4ths e.g G7 resolves up a perfect 4th to C. This resolution 'up a 4th' is in fact the most common movement between chords that you will encounter and you may hear musicians refer to these cadences as 'functional' or 'cyclic'. If you learn the 'cycle' of 4ths, you will have also, inadvertently learned the order of 'flat' key signatures.

The term 'circle' of 5ths actually alludes to an often-used, traditional system of teaching students key signatures: a system which incorporates the use of a circular diagram that introduces each key signature, from C major onwards, in a clockwise fashion. If you learn the 'circle' of 5ths you will have inadvertently learned the order of 'sharp' key signatures.

TRANSPOSING WITH CHORD SYMBOLS

As a musician you will quite often have to transpose songs into other keys. Usually this is in order to make the register more comfortable for a vocalist's range. The end result should be that the chord progression sounds the same, but is either higher or lower in pitch.

The first step in this process is to translate the chords of your original progression into their Roman numeral equivalents. In every major key there are three major chords, three minor chords and one diminished chord, which are always found in the following order: I IIm IIIm IV V VIm VIIdim. While some systems use lowercase numerals for minor and diminished chords, here we are using the more contemporary system commonly used in jazz and popular music. This system uses uppercase numbers for all chords and distinguishes minor chords with a lowercase letter "m" for minor and "dim" for diminished.

CONTINUED

We will start with the 1950s, doo-wop-sounding progression, C Am F G. The first procedure is to give each chord a Roman numeral in the context of the overall key. If you are not sure what key you are in, a good trick is to look for two major chords a tone apart; in this progression we have an F major and a G major chord. Those two chords are almost certainly the IV and V chords, which would make C the I chord. The A minor also fits the key as the VIm chord.

As the chord structure is exactly the same in every key, you can apply the Roman numerals I VIm IV V from any of the 12 possible root notes in the chromatic scale. The table below shows the triads belonging to each key, with the notes of the I, VIm, IV and V chords shown in dark blue.

I	IIm	IIIm	IV	V	VIm	VIIdim
C	Dm	Em	F	G	Am	Bdim
D♭	E♭m	Fm	G♭	A♭	B♭m	Cdim
D	Em	F♯m	G	A	Bm	C♯dim
E♭	Fm	Gm	A♭	B♭	Cm	Ddim
E	F♯m	G♯m	A	B	C♯m	D♯dim
F	Gm	Am	B♭	C	Dm	Edim
F♯	G♯m	A♯m	B	C♯	D♯m	E♯dim
G	Am	Bm	C	D	Em	F♯dim
A♭	B♭m	Cm	D♭	E♭	Fm	Gdim
A	Bm	C♯m	D	E	F♯m	G♯dim
B♭	Cm	Dm	E♭	F	Gm	Adim
B	C♯m	D♯m	E	F♯	G♯m	A♯dim

TRANSPOSING
INSTRUMENTS

Music notation is perceived differently by different musicians based on the instrument that they are playing. Middle C on the treble clef looks the same no matter who you are or what you play; it is shown as a dot on the first ledger line below the stave. If you ask a pianist to play a middle C then you will hear a specific pitch which resonates at 261.6 Hz. Now ask a guitarist to play a middle C and they will play a note which sounds an octave lower than the piano. So musicians who read music are not only learning to recognise the note, but also how to physically play the note on their specific instrument, and the results are not always uniform across the range of instruments available to us.

With some instruments, a C note on a stave translates to a different pitch entirely. Show a middle C to a saxophonist with a tenor sax and the resulting sound you will hear is B♭; give him an alto sax to do the same and you will hear an E♭. To musicians who play 'transposing instruments', dots on a stave represent the fingering to play rather than the actual pitches, and for this reason, their parts should be written in a different key.

The B♭ trumpet sounds a tone lower than written, so parts should be transposed up a tone; from C to D, for example.

The alto sax sounds a major 6th lower than written, so parts should be transposed up the same amount; from C to A, for example.

EXTENDED CHORDS

Triads and tetrads are the foundations of harmony and represent clearly defined chord types which have a specific sound (or function). Major triads and major 7 chords both function as the same thing, although the four-note, major 7 version has a richer sound. The same is true of minor triads and minor 7 chords. Dominant 7 chords can function as a 'static' sound or as functioning V chords. In this chapter we will add more notes to that core group of chords by adding notes above the 7th, otherwise known as extensions.

SIMPLE & COMPOUND INTERVALS

The 12 intervals in the left-hand column in the table below represent every possible chromatic note from any given root note up to one octave. **Intervals smaller than an octave are called 'simple'**. These are the intervals we combine to create chords, arpeggios, scales and modes.

SIMPLE INTERVAL	COMPOUND INTERVAL
♭2	♭9
2	9
#2/♭3	#9
3	10
4	11
#4/♭5	#11
5	–
#5/♭6	♭13
6	13
♭7	–
7	–
OCTAVE	–

The numbers in the right-hand column are compound intervals. These are the same as the simple intervals, but are an octave higher. For example, a major 2nd interval is a tone up from the root note, while a major 9th is an octave plus a major 2nd from the root. Similarly, a minor 13th interval is equivalent to a minor 6th plus an octave from the root note.

The perfect 5th, minor 7th and major 7th can be played an octave higher, but they don't have commonly used, compound-interval names. **An octave is called an octave regardless of which register is used**.

The simple intervals ♯4th/♭5th and ♯5th/♭6th each show two commonly used names for the same interval qualities, but in both cases the compound-interval equivalents are usually only referred to as ♯11th and ♭13th, respectively.

COMPOUND INTERVALS ON THE STAVE

ALL OF the compound intervals are shown on the stave below as melodic intervals from the same root note, C, but can be played from any note. All of these melodic intervals can also be played simultaneously with the root notes, which would make them harmonic intervals. **Another name for certain compound intervals is extensions; this is used when the interval is played in the context of a chord**. All of the compound intervals (or extensions) can be added to triads (e.g. major and minor) and tetrads (e.g. major 7s, minor 7s and dominant 7s).

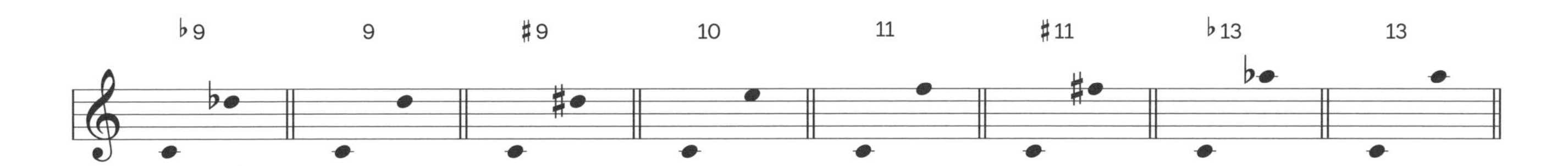

It's a good idea to memorise the following commonly used intervals as they will frequently appear in extended chords.

FIRST OCTAVE	SECOND-OCTAVE EQUIVALENT
2	9
4	11
6	13

EXTENDED CHORDS: 9THS

The three most commonly used four-note chords (tetrads) are major 7, minor 7 and dominant 7. These were originally constructed by harmonising the parent major scale in 3rds to produce the intervals 1 3 5 7 for major 7, 1 ♭3 5 ♭7 for minor 7 and 1 3 5 ♭7 for dominant 7. You can extend a chord beyond the 7th interval by adding another diatonic 3rd on top of these tetrads, which adds a 9th interval. **The stave below shows the three chord types in the key of C with the 9th added**. Notice how the major 9th interval D is the same for every chord, regardless of the chord type.

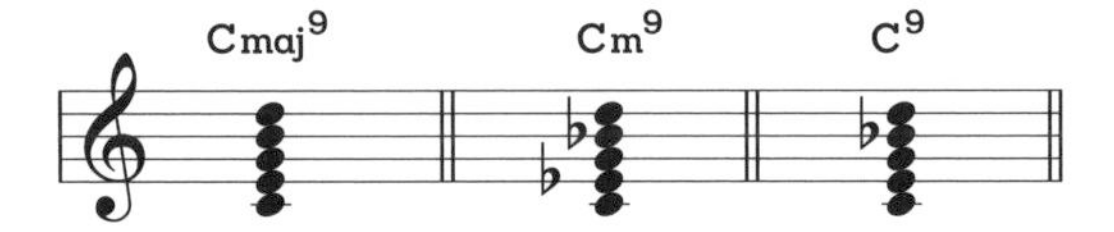

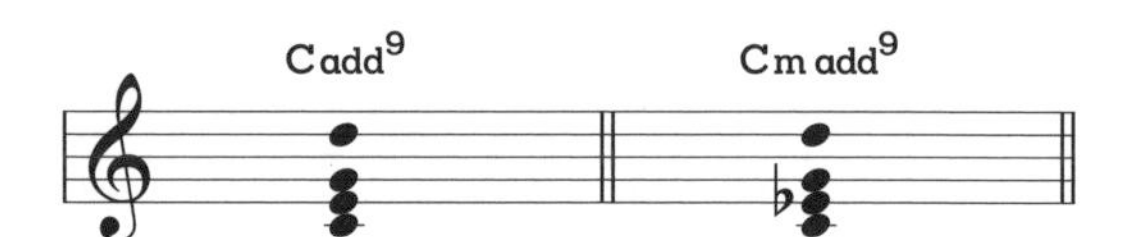

Extended chords are named after the highest interval number present above the 7th. The name 'major 9' suggests that all of the intervals 1 3 5 7 9 are present. However, not all of the notes of an extended chord are essential. In this case, the 5th interval is non-essential, but the 3rd, 7th and 9th are crucial to imparting the chord's harmonic character.

9ths can also be added to major and minor triads. A major triad with a 9th added has the intervals 1 3 5 9. As there is no 7th present, the name 'major 9' does not apply, and 'add 9' is more suitable. The stave on the right shows the C major and minor triads with the added 9th on top.

The table below shows all of the 9th and add 9 chords from the major scale, and their respective intervals. Non-essential intervals are shown in brackets.

CHORD					
MAJOR 9	1	3	(5)	7	9
MINOR 9	1	♭3	(5)	♭7	9
DOMINANT 9	1	3	(5)	♭7	9
MAJOR ADD 9	1	3	5	—	9
MINOR ADD 9	1	♭3	5	—	9

EXTENDED CHORDS: 11THS

Adding another 3rd on top of the 9th interval produces an 11th, which is the equivalent of a 4th plus an octave. Chords with '11' in the name suggest that all of the odd numbered intervals are present. In practice, however, this doesn't always sound good, nor is it always practical to play.

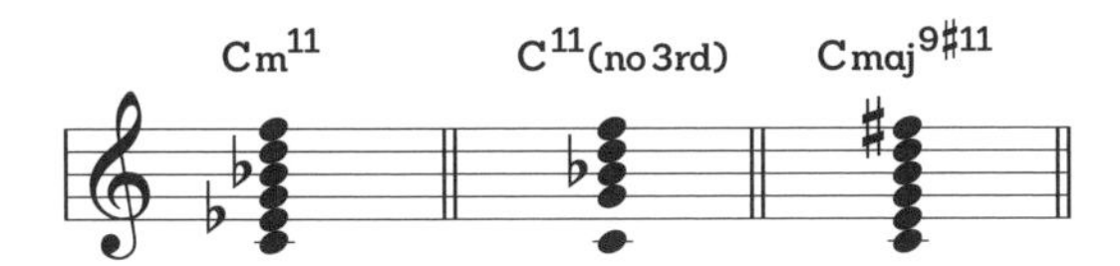

For minor 11 chords, you can play all of the odd-numbered intervals and it will sound fine. The 5th is non-essential, and can be removed. The 9th can also be removed, as the note we are really interested in is the 11th. This leaves the intervals 1 ♭3 ♭7 11, which clearly imply a minor 11 chord when played.

A dominant 11 chord incorporating all of the theoretically correct intervals will sound surprisingly dissonant. This is because a major 3rd and an 11th are a ♭9 interval apart, which is considered to be one of the most dissonant intervals. The solution is to remove the 3rd from the chord, leaving 1 5 ♭7 9 11. Technically, this is no longer a major chord, and is more accurately described as a dominant 9sus4. However, the accepted wisdom is that a dominant 11 is often played with no 3rd.

Major 11 chords have the same problem as dominant 11 chords, as they contain both a 3rd and an 11th interval. Rather than removing the 3rd, the solution in this case is to move the 11th up a semitone to a ♯11. For this reason, the much nicer-sounding C major 9 ♯11 prevails over the major 11.

The following table shows some of the most common 11th chords, and their respective intervals.

CHORD						
MINOR 11	1	♭3	(5)	♭7	9	11
MAJOR 11	1	3	(5)	7	(9)	11
DOMINANT 11	1	—	(5)	♭7	9	11
MAJOR 9♯11	1	3	(5)	7	9	♯11

EXTENDED CHORDS: 13THS

Adding an additional diatonic 3rd on top of the 11 chord produces a 13 chord. A major 13 chord contains the intervals 1 3 5 7 9 11 13, which in the key of C is the notes C E G B D F A. **This is the largest possible chord type, as it already contains every note of the scale, albeit in a different order.** If you want to play all of the notes, all of the rules applicable to 11 chords apply to 13 chords. However, as we have seen with the other extended chords, it is sometimes necessary to remove or adapt notes to make them more practical and pleasant sounding. With 13 chords it is common to remove the 11th. This is especially applicable to the dominant 13, as removing the 11th allows you to keep the 3rd in the chord. Shown below are the minor 13, major 13 and both types of dominant chord: dominant 13 and dominant 13(♯11).

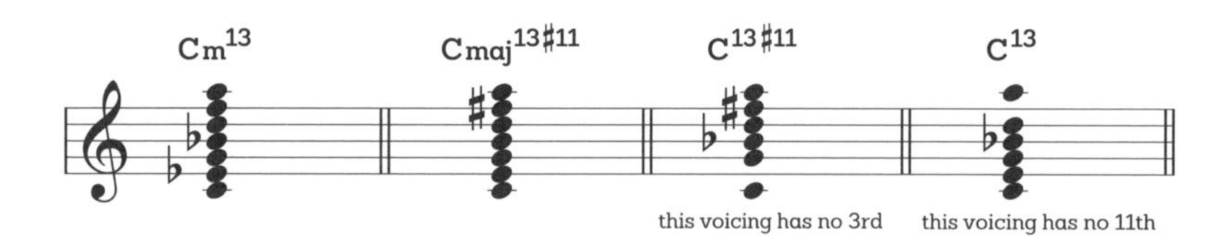

MAJOR 6 AND MINOR 6 CHORDS

SIMILARLY TO the major and minor add 9 chords we saw previously, the 13th interval can be added to a major or minor triad. As there is no 7th present in a triad, however, the additional note does not qualify as an extension above the octave, so is referred to by its simple interval name (i.e. major 6 or minor 6).

MAJOR 6/9 AND MINOR 6/9 CHORDS

IN ADDITION to the 6th interval, a 9th interval can also be added to a major or minor triad to make the rich, open-sounding 6/9 (pronounced 'six-nine') chord. As there is no 7th interval in a major triad, these extra notes are not considered extensions, and technically speaking are simple intervals: 2nd and 6th. By some quirk of chord nomenclature, however, the 2nd is referred to as a 9th, while the 6th remains a 6th. In summary, the 6/9 chord contains the intervals 1 3 5 6 9, and the 5th can be removed without the chord's harmonic character being affected.

The 6 and 6/9 chords are shown below on the stave, with C as their root note.

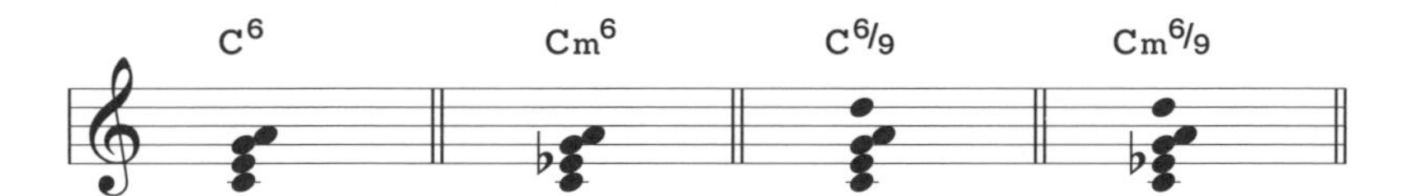

This table summarises the intervals of each chord in this section. In all cases, the 5th is non-essential, and is therefore shown in brackets.

CHORD							
MAJOR 13	1	3	(5)	7	9	(11)	13
MINOR 13	1	♭3	(5)	♭7	9	(11)	13
DOMINANT 13	1	(3)	(5)	♭7	9	(11)	13
MAJOR 13♯11	1	3	(5)	7	9	♯11	13
DOMINANT 13♯11	1	(3)	(5)	♭7	9	♯11	13
MAJOR 6	1	3	(5)	6	—	—	—
MINOR 6	1	♭3	(5)	6	—	—	—
MAJOR 6/9	1	3	(5)	6	9	—	—
MINOR 6/9	1	♭3	(5)	6	9	—	—

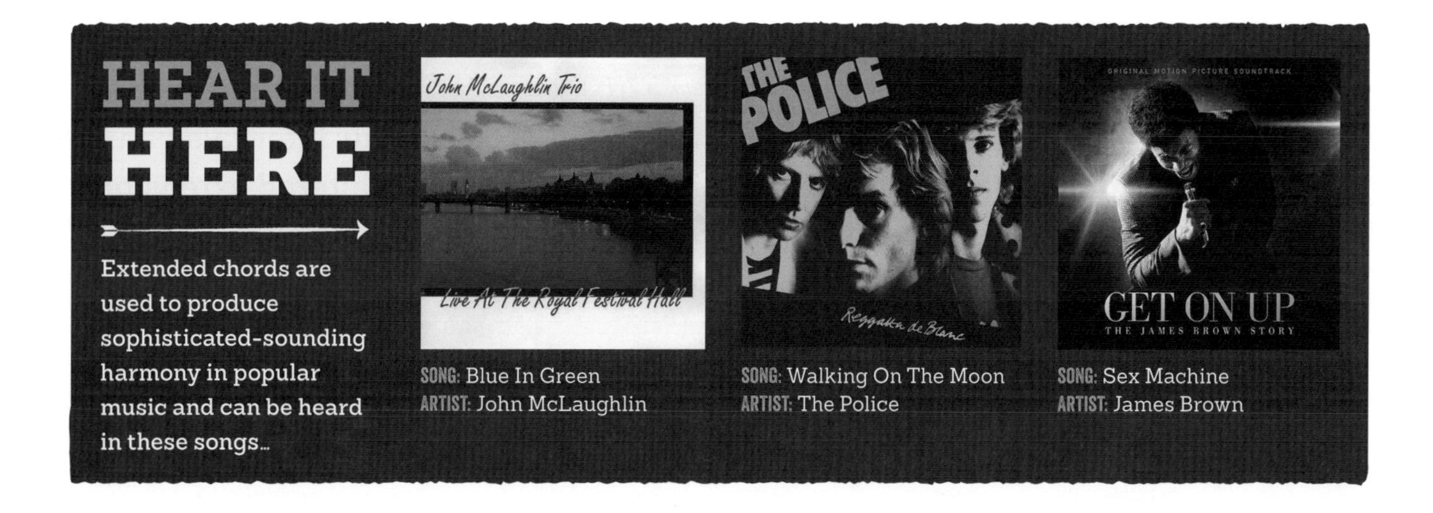

ALTERED CHORDS

Dominant 7 chords are classified in one of two ways: static dominant or functioning dominant. As the name suggests, **a static dominant doesn't move; this could be a James Brown or Chic-style funk groove** that stays on an E9 chord indefinitely. This contradicts the traditional use of a dominant chord (i.e. as a 'functioning dominant' – the 'tense' chord that resolves up a perfect 4th or down a perfect 5th to the tonic). In fact, any dominant chord that's followed by a chord a perfect 4th higher or a perfect 5th lower (i.e. a V7–I cadence) is considered to be a functioning dominant. The inherent tension of a dominant 7 comes from the tritone between its ♭7 and 3rd intervals. By adding altered extensions to the chord, you can increase the tension and make the V7–I much more dramatic – something that jazz musicians do all the time.

'Altered' extensions are so named because they are derived from the altered scale (or 'superlocrian'). This scale is usually spelled in a unique fashion: 1 ♭9 ♯9 3 ♭5 ♯5 ♭7. In the key of C, the scale has the following notes: C D♭ D♯ E G♭ G♯ B♭ C:

Notice that the scale was spelled with reference to 9ths rather than 2nds. This is to show how the scale relates to the chords that it is often used to play over.

The altered scale contains the 1st, 3rd and ♭7th of a dominant 7 chord and the remaining intervals are ♭5th, ♯5th, ♭9th and ♯9th. **Any of these four intervals can be added to the dominant 7 chord to change it into a dominant with altered extensions**. Any combination of those four alterations can be used; however, the ones shown on the stave below are the most common.

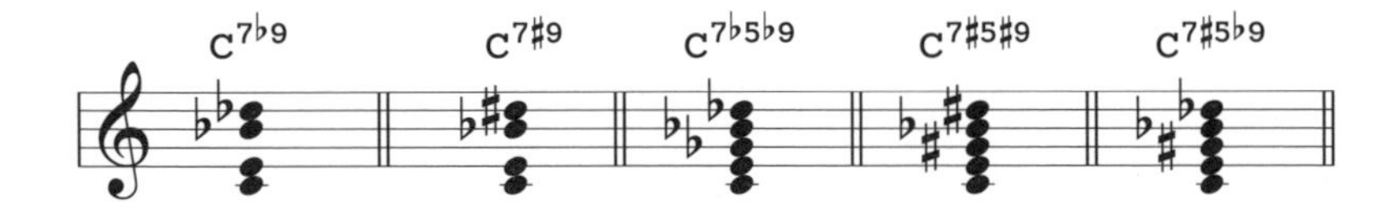

VOICE LEADING

Voice leading is a method of arranging the notes within chords to achieve the smoothest possible route through a progression. This method comes from choral arranging – imagining a choir singing through a chord progression might help you to understand the principles in a practical context.

To keep things simple, we will deal only with triads, but the same method will work for any chords. For example, we will use a I V VIm IV progression in the key of C. First, let's see what those chords look like placed on the stave in root position; this means that the intervals of each chord are 1 3 5 from low to high (see below):

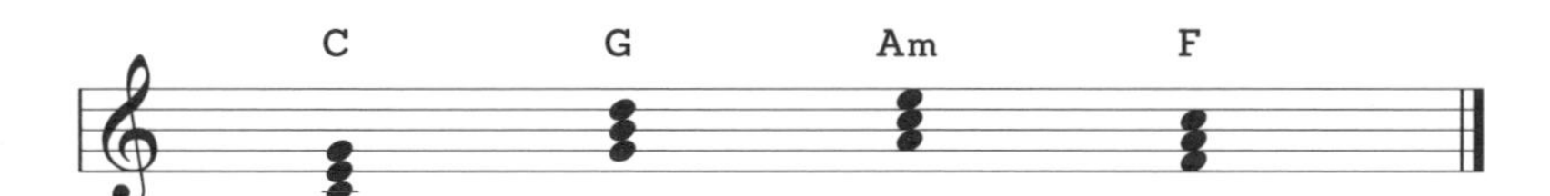

The problem with arranging the notes of the chords like this is the large jumps between chords. The notes between the C and G chords are all 5ths, which is possible, but would not sound smooth when sung by a choir or an *a cappella* trio. The aim is for each individual voice to move as little as possible.

The first thing to do is to spell out each of the chords, looking for common notes between them, i.e. C (C E G), G (G B D), A minor (A C E), F (F A C). You can see that the C, A minor and F chords all contain the note C, so it makes sense that only one vocalist sings that note. Another example is the note G, which appears in both the C chord and the G chord; this note can be sung by a different singer. Other recurring notes are A (A minor and F) and E (C and A minor). This leaves the notes B, D and F, which are played only once each.

Next, we can assign the recurring notes to singers, grouping the closest notes together as shown on the table on page 54.

CONTINUED

ROOT POSITION VOICING	CEG	GBD	ACE	FAC
SINGER 3	G	G	A	A
SINGER 2	E	D	E	F
SINGER 1	C	B	C	C
NEW VOICING	ROOT POSITION	1ST INVERSION	1ST INVERSION	2ND INVERSION

The resulting four chords are played as root, 1st and 2nd inversions. Finally, if we place those inversions on the stave we can see there is much less movement between chords compared to the original version. This should sound much smoother and more refined.

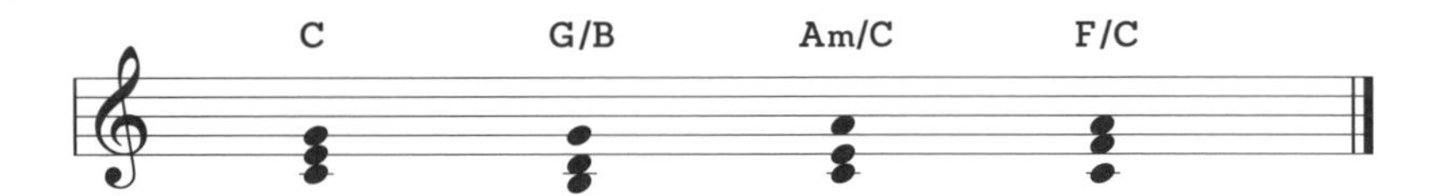

WHY IT MATTERS

Writing music for several instruments is a tricky business. All the notes of all the parts might technically fit your chord progression and yet the music can still sound awkward and clunky if no attention has been paid to voice leading. If you are happy that the actual chord sequence works, play through each part individually and look at the horizontal lines as each part moves from one note to the next. If you really need to move from one harmony part to another with a larger interval, consider adding bridging notes (called passing notes) to avoid jerky-sounding parts and keep the lines smooth.

BAND KNOWLEDGE

This chapter expands on the introduction to the common instruments in rock and pop bands and their notation, which featured in Rockschool's Popular Music Theory Guidebook 1. You will learn the more advanced notation used for vocals, guitar, bass, drums and keys. This is followed by a guide to brass and string instruments used occasionally in popular music and an introduction to how they are notated.

ADVANCED NOTATION ROCK BAND

Most of the instrument-specific notation and techniques used by drums, guitar, bass guitar, vocals and keys were covered in Book 1 of this series. In Grades 6 to 8, some more advanced techniques are introduced. A summary of these, together with notation and a description of each technique, are outlined below.

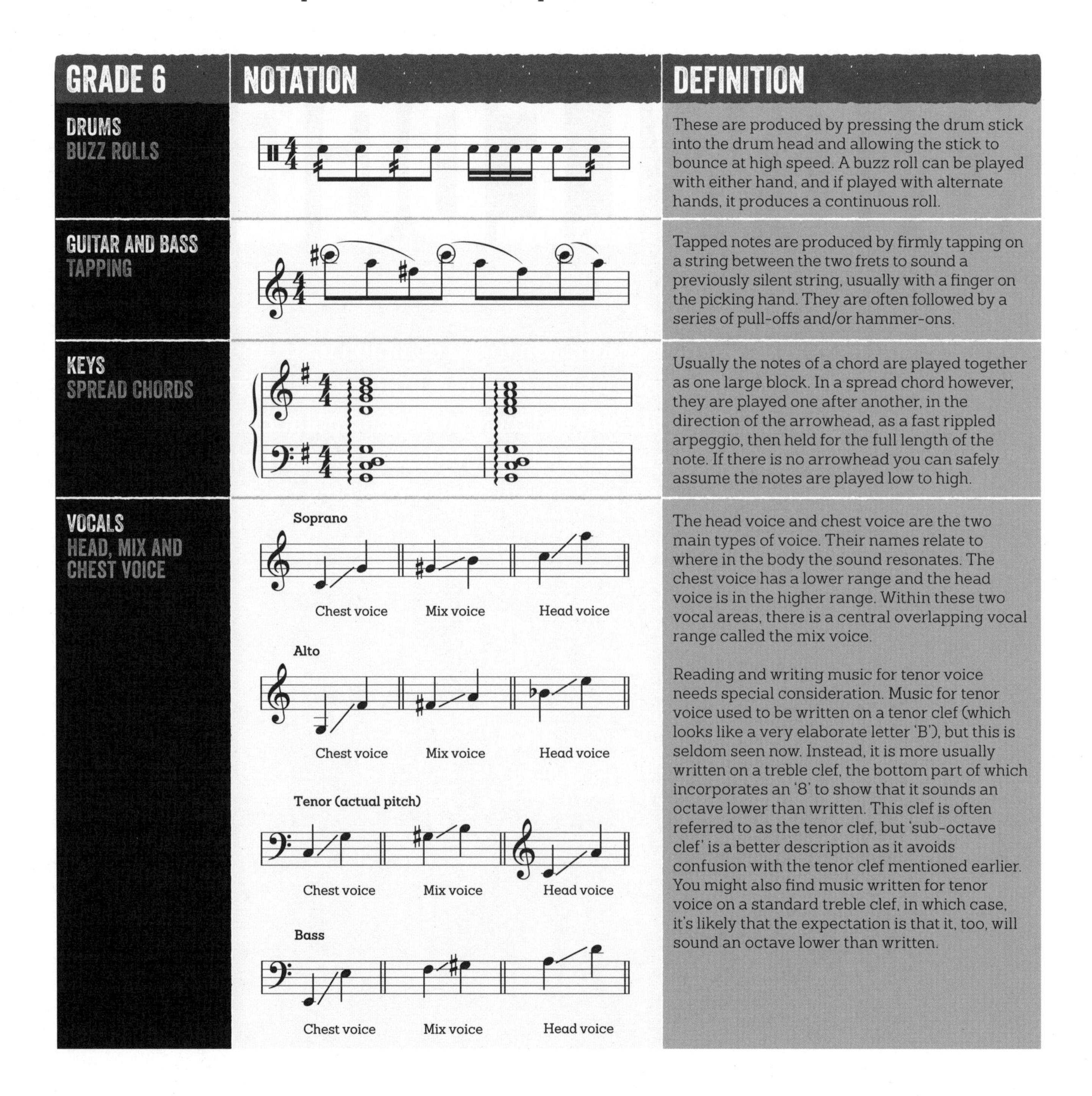

GRADE 6	NOTATION	DEFINITION
DRUMS BUZZ ROLLS		These are produced by pressing the drum stick into the drum head and allowing the stick to bounce at high speed. A buzz roll can be played with either hand, and if played with alternate hands, it produces a continuous roll.
GUITAR AND BASS TAPPING		Tapped notes are produced by firmly tapping on a string between the two frets to sound a previously silent string, usually with a finger on the picking hand. They are often followed by a series of pull-offs and/or hammer-ons.
KEYS SPREAD CHORDS		Usually the notes of a chord are played together as one large block. In a spread chord however, they are played one after another, in the direction of the arrowhead, as a fast rippled arpeggio, then held for the full length of the note. If there is no arrowhead you can safely assume the notes are played low to high.
VOCALS HEAD, MIX AND CHEST VOICE	Soprano: Chest voice, Mix voice, Head voice Alto: Chest voice, Mix voice, Head voice Tenor (actual pitch): Chest voice, Mix voice, Head voice Bass: Chest voice, Mix voice, Head voice	The head voice and chest voice are the two main types of voice. Their names relate to where in the body the sound resonates. The chest voice has a lower range and the head voice is in the higher range. Within these two vocal areas, there is a central overlapping vocal range called the mix voice. Reading and writing music for tenor voice needs special consideration. Music for tenor voice used to be written on a tenor clef (which looks like a very elaborate letter 'B'), but this is seldom seen now. Instead, it is more usually written on a treble clef, the bottom part of which incorporates an '8' to show that it sounds an octave lower than written. This clef is often referred to as the tenor clef, but 'sub-octave clef' is a better description as it avoids confusion with the tenor clef mentioned earlier. You might also find music written for tenor voice on a standard treble clef, in which case, it's likely that the expectation is that it, too, will sound an octave lower than written.

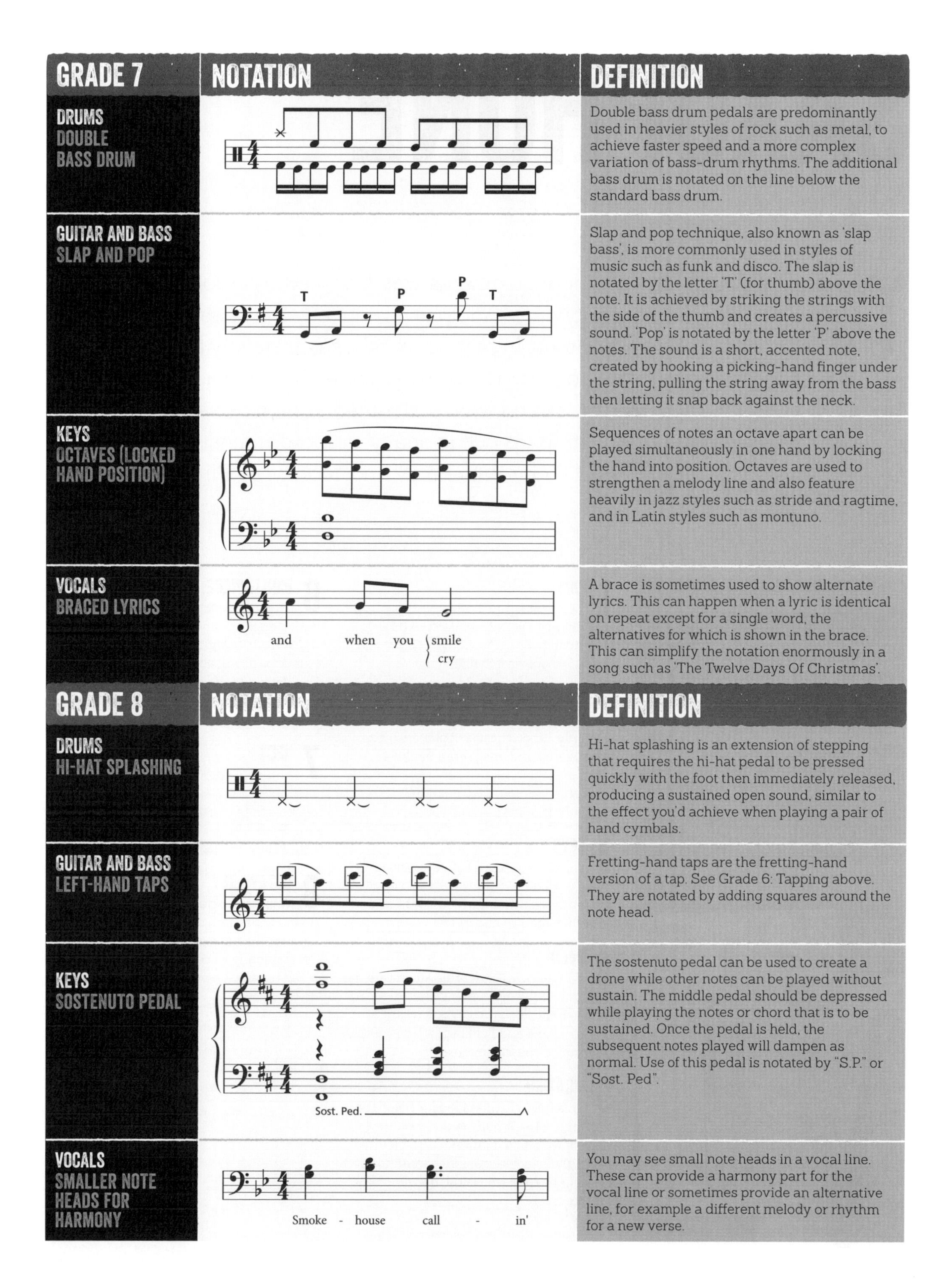

GRADE 7	NOTATION	DEFINITION
DRUMS DOUBLE BASS DRUM		Double bass drum pedals are predominantly used in heavier styles of rock such as metal, to achieve faster speed and a more complex variation of bass-drum rhythms. The additional bass drum is notated on the line below the standard bass drum.
GUITAR AND BASS SLAP AND POP	T P P T	Slap and pop technique, also known as 'slap bass', is more commonly used in styles of music such as funk and disco. The slap is notated by the letter 'T' (for thumb) above the note. It is achieved by striking the strings with the side of the thumb and creates a percussive sound. 'Pop' is notated by the letter 'P' above the notes. The sound is a short, accented note, created by hooking a picking-hand finger under the string, pulling the string away from the bass then letting it snap back against the neck.
KEYS OCTAVES (LOCKED HAND POSITION)		Sequences of notes an octave apart can be played simultaneously in one hand by locking the hand into position. Octaves are used to strengthen a melody line and also feature heavily in jazz styles such as stride and ragtime, and in Latin styles such as montuno.
VOCALS BRACED LYRICS	and when you {smile / cry}	A brace is sometimes used to show alternate lyrics. This can happen when a lyric is identical on repeat except for a single word, the alternatives for which is shown in the brace. This can simplify the notation enormously in a song such as 'The Twelve Days Of Christmas'.

GRADE 8	NOTATION	DEFINITION
DRUMS HI-HAT SPLASHING		Hi-hat splashing is an extension of stepping that requires the hi-hat pedal to be pressed quickly with the foot then immediately released, producing a sustained open sound, similar to the effect you'd achieve when playing a pair of hand cymbals.
GUITAR AND BASS LEFT-HAND TAPS		Fretting-hand taps are the fretting-hand version of a tap. See Grade 6: Tapping above. They are notated by adding squares around the note head.
KEYS SOSTENUTO PEDAL	Sost. Ped.	The sostenuto pedal can be used to create a drone while other notes can be played without sustain. The middle pedal should be depressed while playing the notes or chord that is to be sustained. Once the pedal is held, the subsequent notes played will dampen as normal. Use of this pedal is notated by "S.P." or "Sost. Ped".
VOCALS SMALLER NOTE HEADS FOR HARMONY	Smoke - house call - in'	You may see small note heads in a vocal line. These can provide a harmony part for the vocal line or sometimes provide an alternative line, for example a different melody or rhythm for a new verse.

SAXOPHONE

The saxophone family of wind instruments was invented by Adolphe Sax in the 1840s. Of the many saxophones Adolphe produced, the most common are soprano, alto, tenor and baritone. In popular music, sax is mostly associated with jazz, funk, soul and reggae, as groups in those genres often have horn sections (small groups of musicians who play brass and wind instruments, such as sax, trumpet and trombone). However, sax does crop up occasionally in more mainstream rock and pop (e.g. 'Last Friday Night (T.G.I.F.)' by Katy Perry and 'Money' by Pink Floyd).

DIFFERENCES IN SAXOPHONES

The most commonly used saxes are soprano, alto, tenor and baritone. Soprano is used most often as a lead instrument owing to its eerie, melancholic sound, which makes it ideal for solos in ballads. Alto sounds punchy, with a wider, heavier sound than soprano. Tenor is mostly associated with jazz, with its fat and full sound (sometimes described as 'smoky'). Baritone has a loud, percussive lower register (it's the lowest-pitched sax) and is typically used as part of a horn section.

1 BODY

The saxophone's body consists of a straight main section called the tube, a U-shaped bend at the bottom (bow) and a flared 'output' end (bell).

2 TONE HOLES

A range of 20 to 23 holes are cut into the body. When the sax is played, these are covered and uncovered by the keys in various combinations to shorten and lengthen the 'pipe', thus changing the pitch of the notes.

3 KEYS

The keys (or cups) are the player-operated 'buttons' that cover and uncover the tone holes, making an airtight seal with their leather pads when closed.

4 REED

The reed, which vibrates to create the raw tone of the instrument when gripped between the lips and blown through, is made of cane and held in place within the mouthpiece by the ligature.

5 LIGATURE

This (usually) metal collar holds the reed of the saxophone in place on the mouthpiece. The ligature has to be fitted and tightened with care so it maintains its grip on the reed while still allowing it to vibrate freely.

6 MOUTHPIECE

The mouthpiece is mounted over the cork ring at the end of the neck. It can be made from a range of materials, including plastic, vulcanised rubber and bronze. The design of the mouthpiece has a significant effect on the sound of the instrument.

7 NECK

This is the bent top section of the saxophone's tubing that terminates at the neck cork, to which the mouthpiece connects. The neck also contains the octave key and its tone hole.

8 OCTAVE KEY

When the octave key is pressed (using the thumb of the player's left hand), it opens the uppermost tone hole and consequently raises the register of the sax by an octave. The octave key is positioned on the neck.

ALTO SAX

ALONG WITH the tenor sax, alto is the most likely of the saxophone family to show up in popular music. Jazz is its most natural home, and famous jazz musicians who have played alto include Charlie Parker, Cannonball Adderley and Eric Dolphy.

SOPRANO SAX

The soprano sax is easily recognisable thanks to its straight body and neck, and distinctive sound. It is arguably more difficult to play in tune than other saxes, and the quality of its tone varies depending on the ability of the player. Kenny G is the best-known soprano saxophonist in rock and pop music.

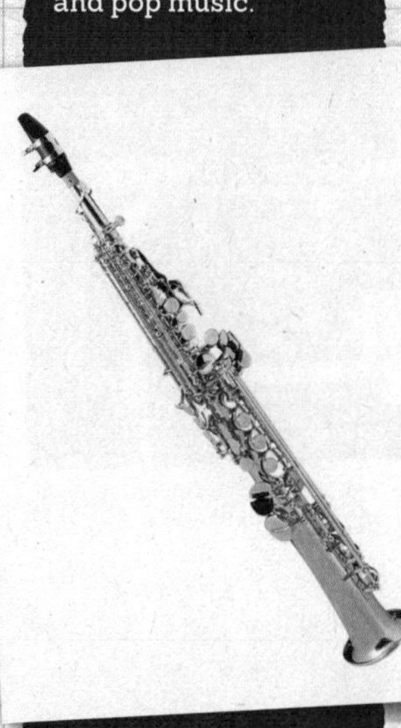

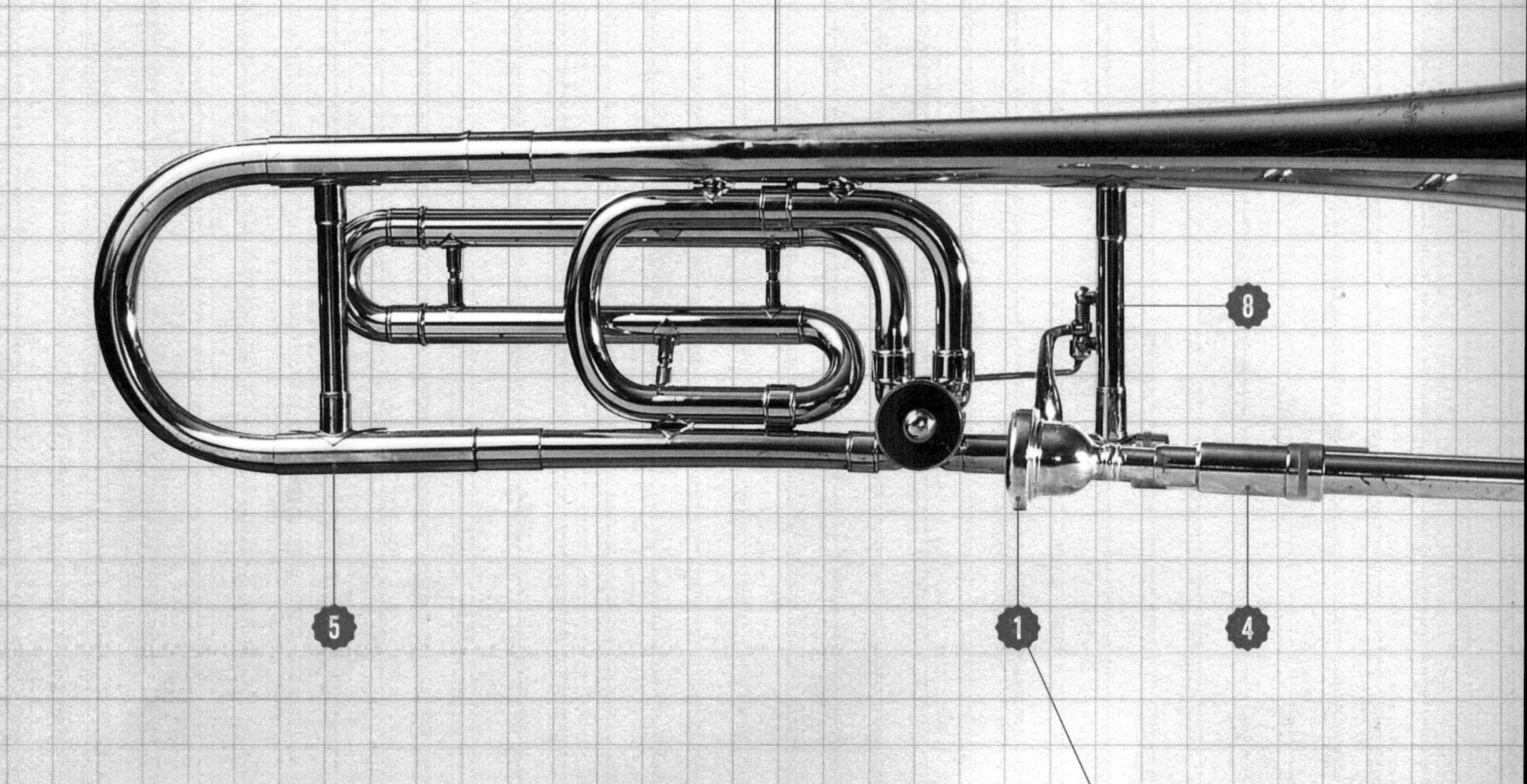

TROMBONE

The name trombone comes from the Italian word meaning 'large trumpet'. However, unlike a trumpet, which uses keys to produce different notes, the trombone uses a slide. There are two types, tenor and bass, of which tenor is the more common. Both are the same length, but the bass trombone has a larger bell to help produce its deeper, richer tone. The trombone is occasionally used as a solo instrument for effect in pop and dance records ('Well, Well, Well' by Duffy), but more often features as part of a horn section, for example, in jazz, ska and funk.

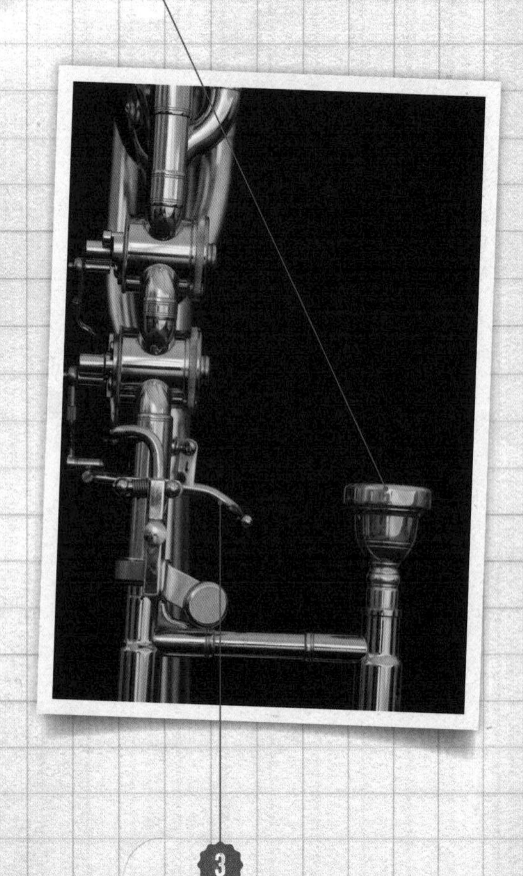

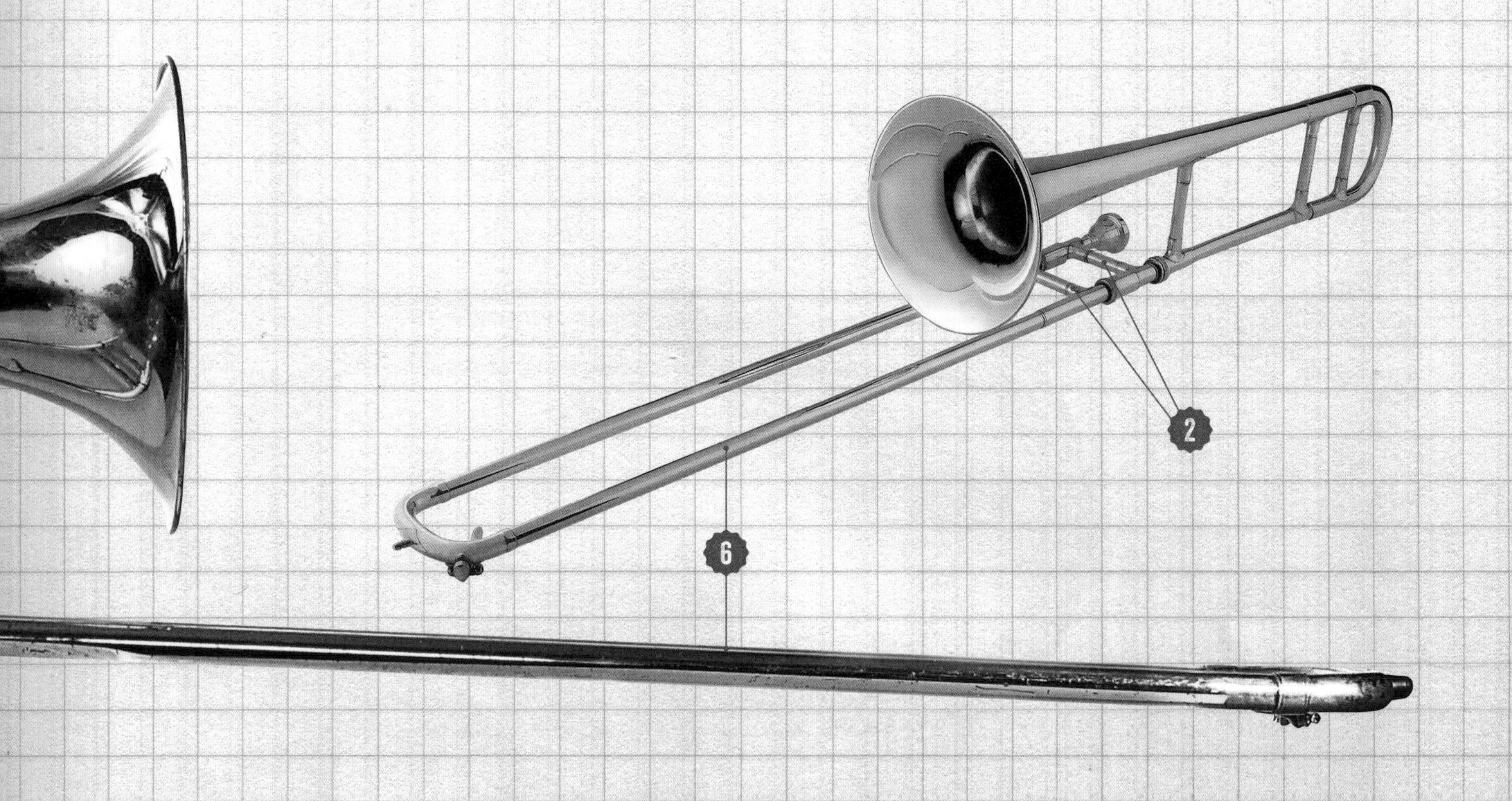

1 MOUTHPIECE

The raw tone of the trombone is created by the lips of the player making an air-tight seal with the mouthpiece and being forcibly 'buzzed' by the player to vibrate the column of air within the instrument. The mouthpiece itself varies hugely in terms of size, shape and material composition.

2 FIRST AND SECOND BRACE

Also known as first and second stay, the braces are two fixed sections of tubing soldered to the slide that the player holds with the fingers of both hands in order to facilitate movement of the slide in and out.

3 TRIGGER

This thumb-operated valve found on the tenor trombone is used to lower the fundamental pitch of the instrument from B♭ to F. Bass trombones add to this with a second trigger, which enables the low B to be played.

4 SLIDE RECEIVER

The slide receiver is the collar at the end of the bell section into which the slide is inserted. A 'lock nut' is used to keep the bell and slide from separating.

5 TUNING SLIDE

The tuning slide is a section of tubing forming the crook between the neck and the bell that can be slid in and out, altering the pipe length of the trombone and changing its overall tuning. Some trombones use an alternative mechanism.

6 HAND SLIDE

The hand slide slides in and out of the bell section to change the length of the tubing and the column of air within, thus modulating the pitch of the note heard when the mouthpiece is blown correctly.

7 BELL SECTION

Made of brass, the bell section is the curved tube that extends from the slide receiver to the flared end of the trombone, from which the sound is emitted. In the playing position the bell section rests on the shoulder of the trombonist.

8 BELL BRACE

The bell brace is a 'cross-bar' which secures the two lengths of the bell section, maintaining the rigidity of the whole assembly. If the trombone is of the trigger-less type, the player's left thumb rests on the bell brace.

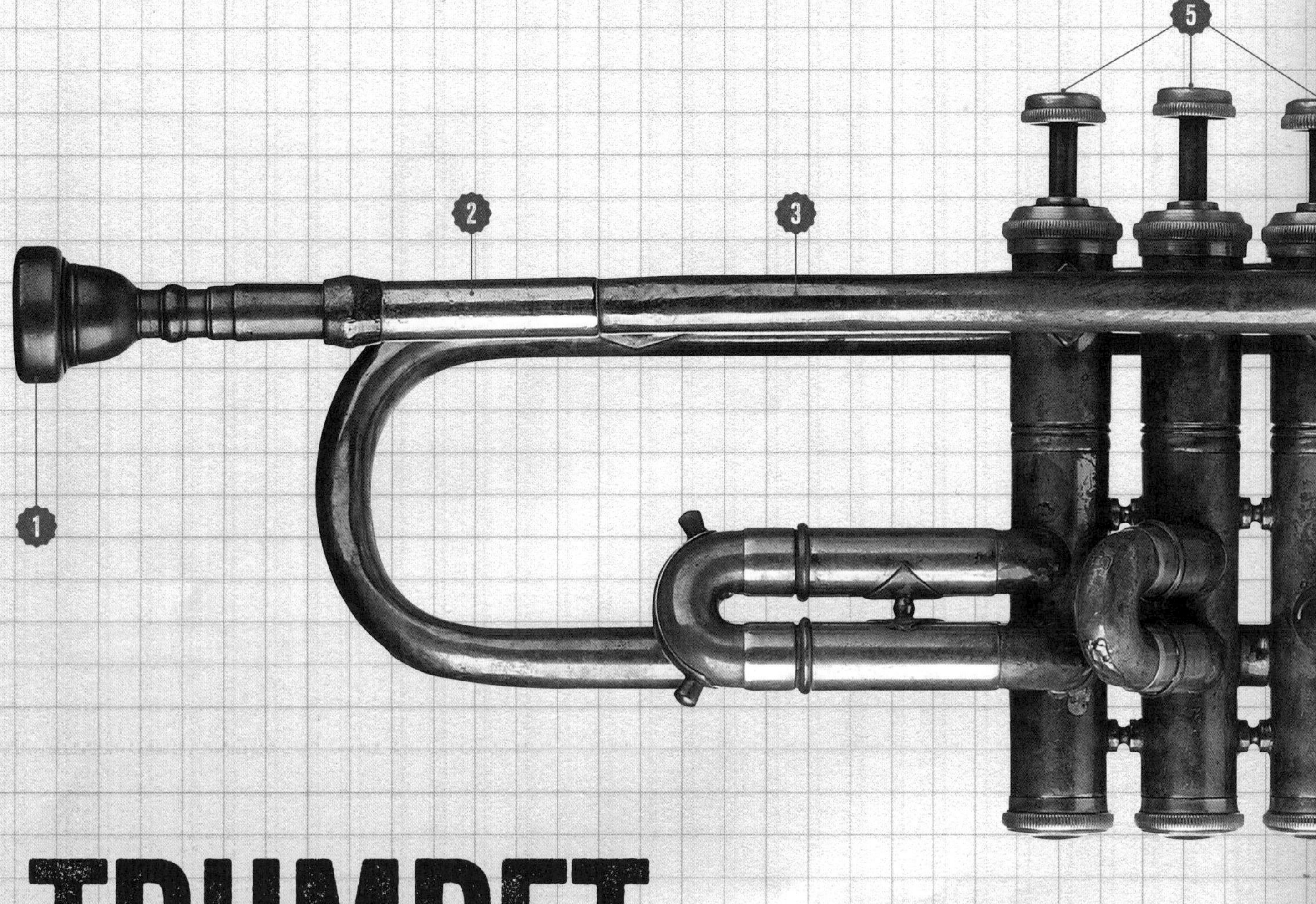

TRUMPET

The lineage of the trumpet can be traced back to some of the world's oldest instruments; its primitive ancestors date back to Neolithic times. Don't be fooled by the small size or the simplistic-seeming, three-keyed design, though – players have developed a variety of complex tongue and mouth techniques which, in combination with different fingerings of the valves, enable a range of effects. Whether it's in the hands of virtuoso jazz soloists such as Louis Armstrong, Miles Davis and Dizzy Gillespie, or punching out the stabs and high-melody lines in the horn sections of Motown, funk and old-school R&B hits, the trumpet is one of music's most versatile instruments.

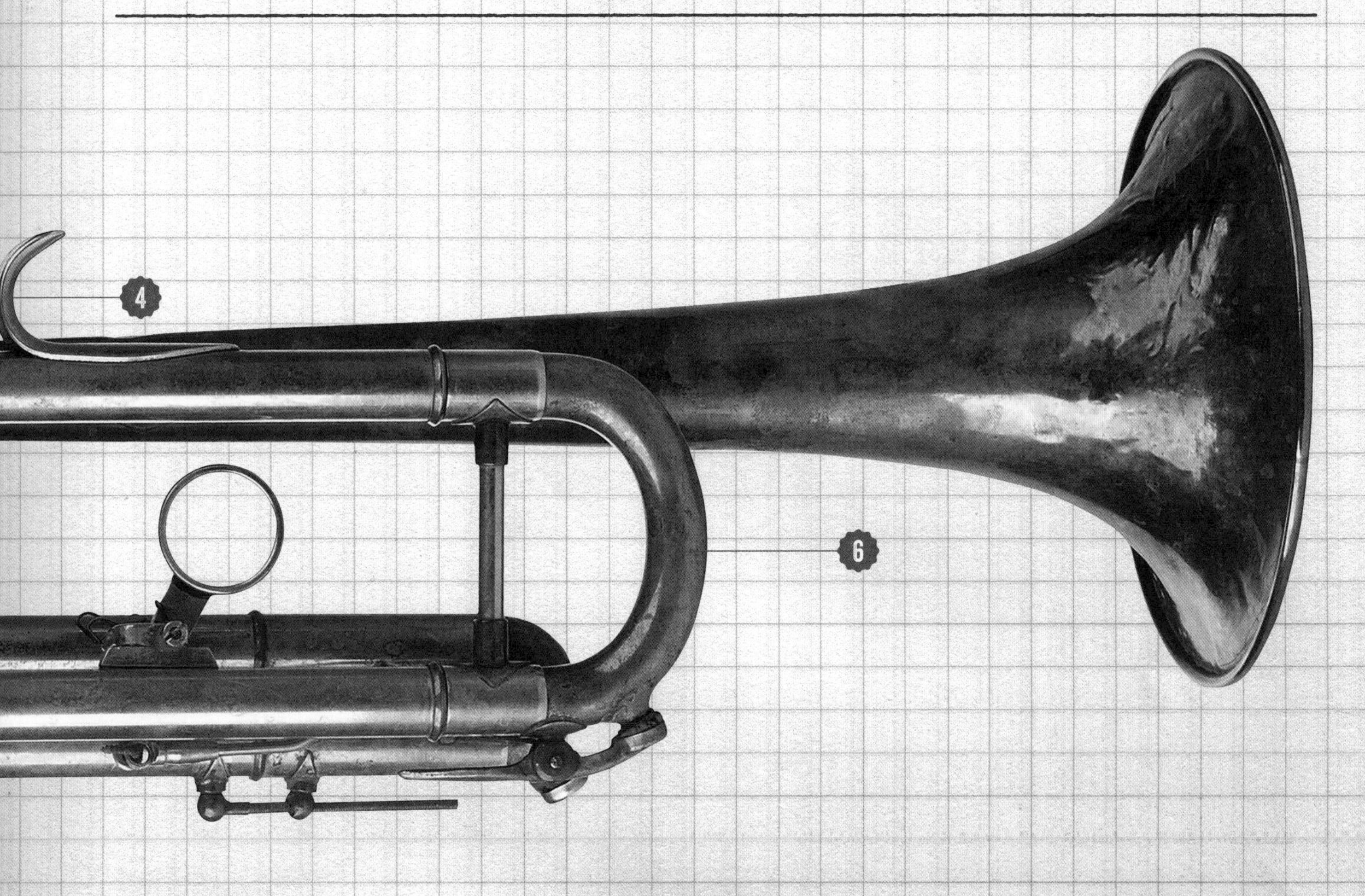

1 MOUTHPIECE

The fundamental sound of the trumpet is created by the player rapidly oscillating their lips on the mouthpiece to produce a 'buzzing' sound which vibrates the column of air contained inside the tubing. As is the case with all brass instruments, the shape and size of the mouthpiece directly influence the tone.

2 MOUTHPIECE RECEIVER

This brass cylinder is soldered to the end of the leadpipe, into which the mouthpiece is inserted. The annulus – the gap between the end of the mouthpiece and the start of the leadpipe – has a profound effect on the playability and pitching of the instrument.

3 LEADPIPE

The section of tubing extending from the mouthpiece receiver to the tuning slide is known as the leadpipe. This is fixed in place in most trumpets, although piccolo models feature interchangeable leadpipes, enabling them to play in the keys of B♭ and A.

4 FINGER HOOK

A metal hook attached to the leadpipe, next to the valves, the finger hook gives the trumpeter the ability to play the trumpet with just one hand, leaving the other free – handy for changing a mute, or turning the pages of a score.

5 VALVES

The three valves of the trumpet are used to route the airflow through the valve slides, increasing the length of the air column and lowering the pitch of the note played. The extent of this lowering depends on the combination of valves depressed at the time.

6 TUNING SLIDE

The overall tuning of the trumpet is adjusted using the main tuning slide at the end of the leadpipe – it is pushed in to shorten the air column (raising the pitch) and out to lengthen it (lowering the pitch).

7 BELL

The bell is the flared end of the trumpet, from which the sound emanates. Although the bell is made of brass, it is often lacquered in silver or gold to produce different sonic characteristics, and its shape is highly influential on the tone of the instrument. Some trumpets feature a sliding bell (called a tuning bell) for further tuning.

NOTATION GUIDE HORNS

In contemporary music, the term 'horn section' describes two or more players commonly playing a mixture of brass instruments such as trumpets and trombones, and reed instruments such as saxophones. Horn sections can be made up of any combination, but there are some common formats. A typical two-piece horn section would be made up of a trumpet and a tenor saxophone. Popular three-piece horn-section line-ups include trumpet, tenor saxophone and tenor trombone, or trumpet, tenor and baritone saxophone. Four-piece horn sections often feature two trumpets, tenor sax and trombone. All horns are transposing instruments, notated in treble clef – apart from the tenor and bass trombone, both of which are non-transposing, and are notated in bass clef.

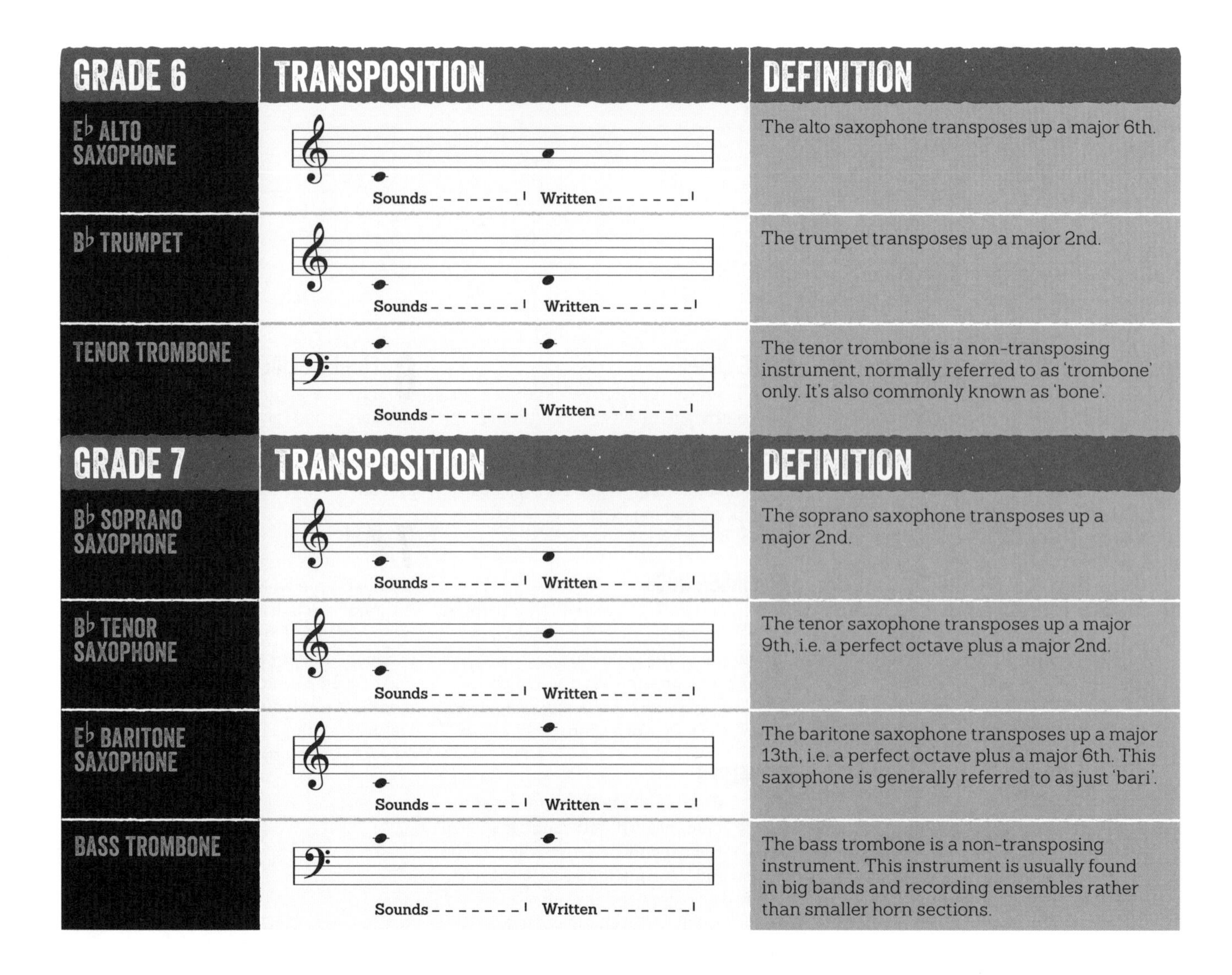

GRADE 6	TRANSPOSITION	DEFINITION
E♭ ALTO SAXOPHONE	Sounds - - - - - - - Written - - - - - - -	The alto saxophone transposes up a major 6th.
B♭ TRUMPET	Sounds - - - - - - - Written - - - - - - -	The trumpet transposes up a major 2nd.
TENOR TROMBONE	Sounds - - - - - - - Written - - - - - - -	The tenor trombone is a non-transposing instrument, normally referred to as 'trombone' only. It's also commonly known as 'bone'.
GRADE 7	**TRANSPOSITION**	**DEFINITION**
B♭ SOPRANO SAXOPHONE	Sounds - - - - - - - Written - - - - - - -	The soprano saxophone transposes up a major 2nd.
B♭ TENOR SAXOPHONE	Sounds - - - - - - - Written - - - - - - -	The tenor saxophone transposes up a major 9th, i.e. a perfect octave plus a major 2nd.
E♭ BARITONE SAXOPHONE	Sounds - - - - - - - Written - - - - - - -	The baritone saxophone transposes up a major 13th, i.e. a perfect octave plus a major 6th. This saxophone is generally referred to as just 'bari'.
BASS TROMBONE	Sounds - - - - - - - Written - - - - - - -	The bass trombone is a non-transposing instrument. This instrument is usually found in big bands and recording ensembles rather than smaller horn sections.

SMALL HORN ARRANGEMENT

THIS TWO-BAR melody shows the same short phrase transposed according to each instrument's requirements. Note that the key signatures have changed with the transposition; the original melody is in the key of B♭ major. The B♭ transposing instruments are in the key of C major (soprano saxophone, tenor saxophone and trumpet) and the E♭ transposing instruments are in the key of G major (alto saxophone, baritone saxophone). The tenor trombone and bass trombone are in the same key, as they are non-transposing instruments.

HORN RANGES

THE RANGES illustrated are used in Rockschool popular music theory exams, and represent a range achievable by most horn players. As with other pitched instruments, more advanced players may be able to play higher notes than shown here.

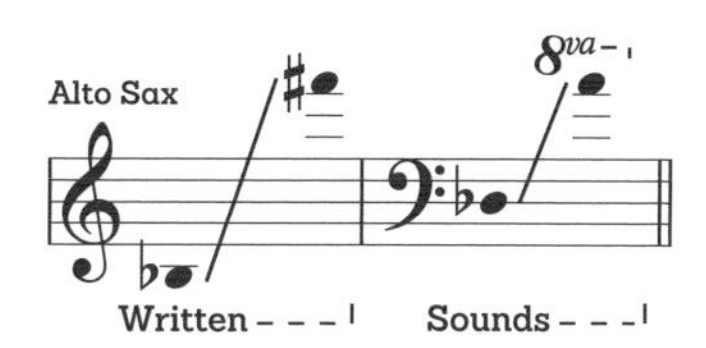

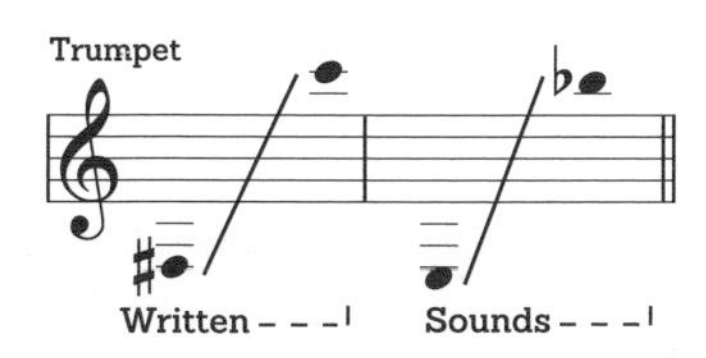

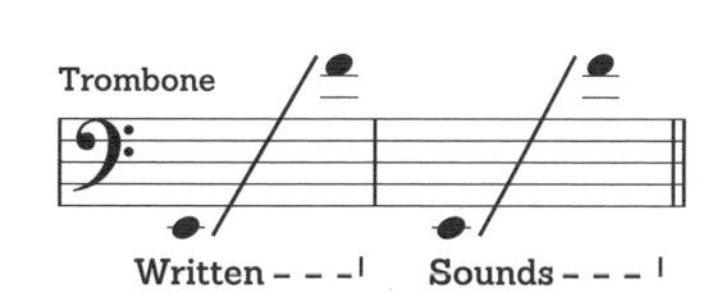

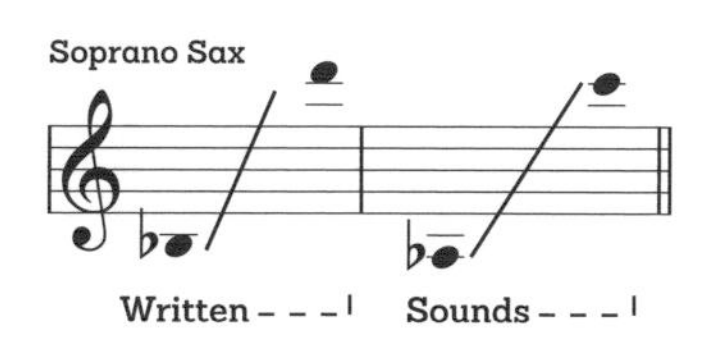

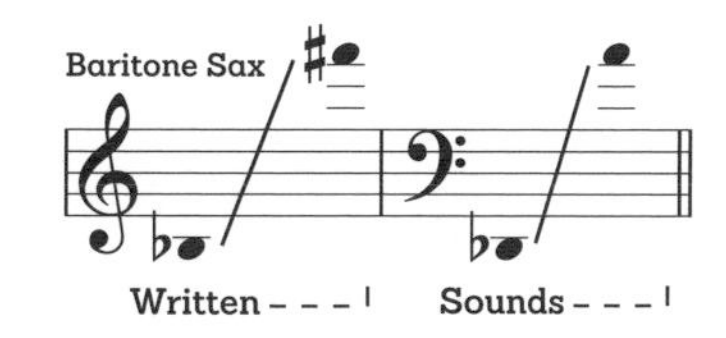

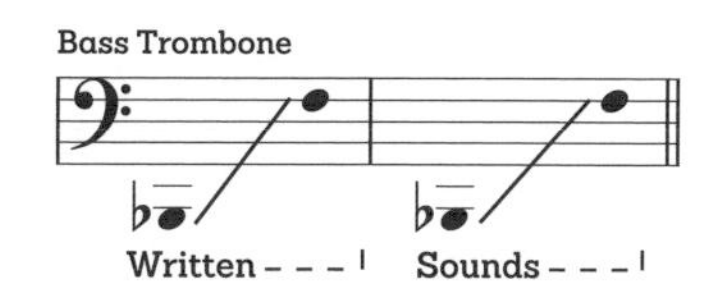

VIOLIN/VIOLA

The violin, together with its lower-pitched, slightly larger-sized counterpart, the viola, are both (predominantly) bowed string instruments that have crossed over from the world of classical music to fulfil a role in the realm of rock, pop and other genres. The use of string sections re-emerged in popular music in the 1960s and 1970s, and the violin has played its part in everything from the swirl of '70s disco and tugging the heartstrings in pop ballads, to providing the drama of symphonic metal and the sonic experiments of avant-garde musicians. The instrument's central role in folk music remains undiminished, and contemporary artists such as Andrew Bird have expanded its expressive possibilities by using looper pedals and other electronic effects.

1 TUNING PEGS

Directly below the (purely decorative) scroll sits the peg box, a hollowed-out space in which the tuning pegs are housed. Each of the four strings is wound round its own peg, and turning a peg tightens or loosens that string, raising or lowering its pitch.

2 NECK AND FINGERBOARD

The (traditionally) ebony fingerboard of the violin is mounted on the (typically) maple neck, and is where the strings are 'stopped' by the violinist to control their pitch when bowed or plucked. The fingerboard is gently concave along its length, with a very specific convex curve across its width.

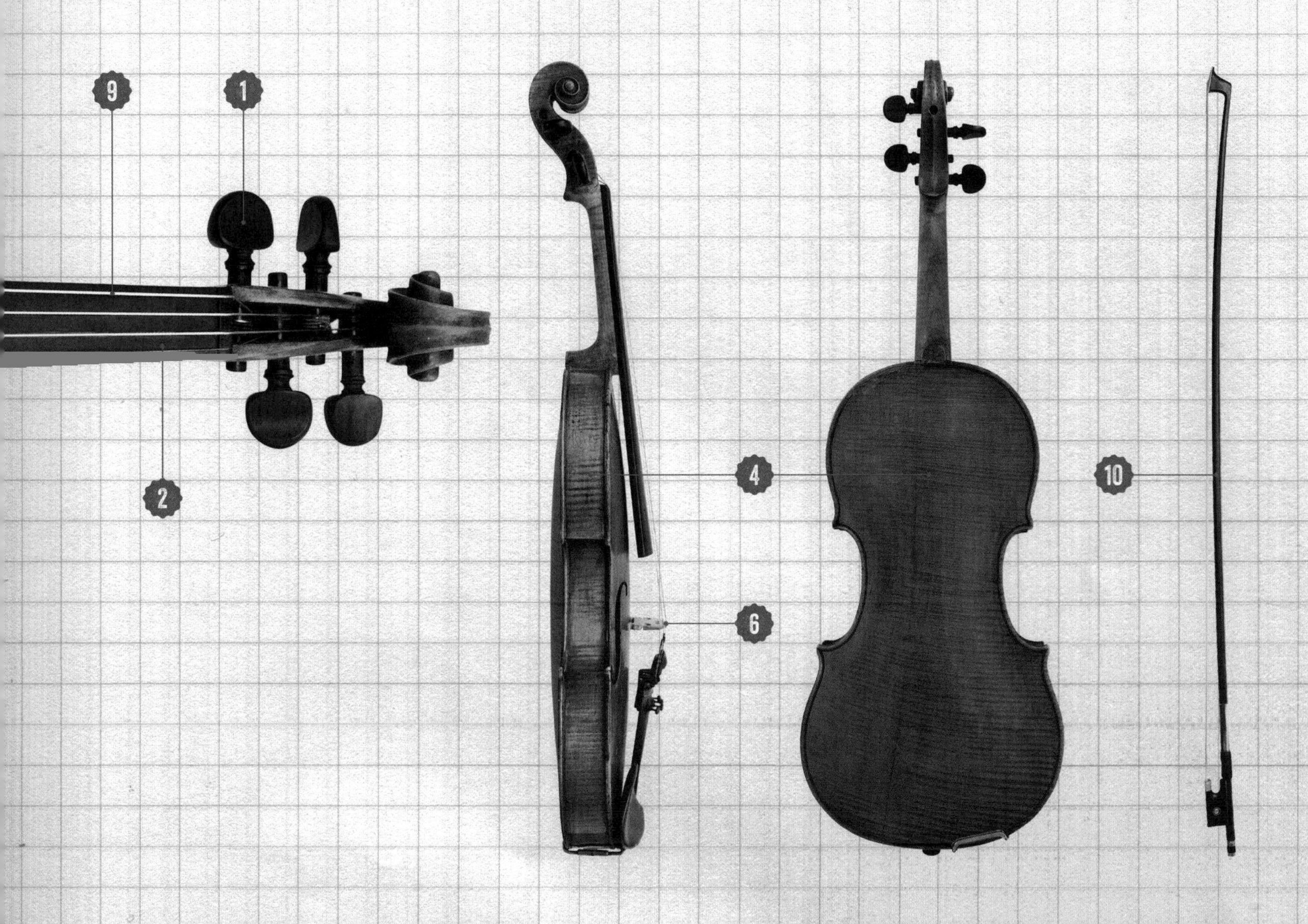

3 SOUNDBOARD

The spruce top surface of the violin, also known as the 'belly', resonates in sympathy with the strings, which pass their vibrations to it via the bridge. The soundboard also transmits the vibrations to the maple back of the violin, via the internal sound post and bass bar (not shown).

4 BODY

Together, the soundboard, back and the 'wall' between them, the ribs, make up the hourglass-shaped body of the violin. Comprising the upper bout, lower bout and waist, the body amplifies the vibrations of the strings via the bridge, and defines the tone of the instrument.

5 F-HOLES

The two F-shaped cutouts on either side of the bridge serve two sonic purposes: helping the soundboard to resonate freely, and providing an exit port for some of the soundwaves oscillating within the body, both of which aid the projection of sound.

6 BRIDGE

The maple bridge provides the lower tension point for the vibrating section of the strings (the upper tension point being the nut, just below the pegs) and transmits string vibration to the soundboard, which resonates in sympathy. Below the bridge, inside the body, are the sound post and bass bar, which transmit the soundboard vibrations to the back of the violin.

7 CHIN REST

This attachment (along with the optional shoulder rest) makes it easier to hold the violin between the chin and collarbone. Using a chin rest alleviates the need for the left hand to bear the weight of the instrument, freeing it up fully for the more important role of stopping the strings.

8 TAILPIECE

This piece of wood at the bottom of the violin is where the strings are anchored. One or more fine-tuner screws are built into the tailpiece, allowing for more precise tensioning of the strings than is possible using the pegs alone.

9 STRINGS

The four strings of the violin are generally tuned to perfect 5ths (from low to high: G, D, A and E); the viola's slightly heavier strings are tuned a 5th below (from low to high: C, G, D and A). Strings are made of metal wound around a synthetic or metal core, or the traditional 'catgut' (actually sheep intestine). Each type of string composition has its own characteristic sound.

10 BOW

The bow consists of a wooden shaft called the stick with a point at one end (the tip) and a brass nut at the other. A length of horsehair is tensioned between the tip and a wooden block (the frog) by the nut. Adjusting the nut moves the frog backwards or forwards, which increases or decreases the tension of the hair. When the bow is rubbed across the strings it causes them to vibrate, resonating the body of the violin via the bridge and generating sound. In order to promote friction, rosin (a resin derived from pines and other plants) needs to be regularly applied to the horsehair.

CELLO/ DOUBLE BASS

The double bass and its slightly smaller sibling, the cello, are large-scale fretless orchestral instruments adopted by a variety of genres of popular music. The cello is primarily played with a bow, whereas rockabilly and jazz musicians, by plucking and slapping the strings, have taken full advantage of the percussive qualities of the double bass. The mournful low register of the cello is often likened to the human voice, and has featured in all kinds of pop music since the 1960s, when bands such as The Beatles popularised its sound. The versatile double bass has become a staple of jazz, blues, rock 'n' roll, bluegrass and many other styles.

1 TUNING PEGS

Directly below the (purely decorative) scroll sits the peg box, a hollowed-out space in which the tuning pegs are housed. Each of the four strings is wound round its own peg, and turning a peg tightens or loosens that string, raising or lowering its pitch.

2 NECK AND FINGERBOARD

The (traditionally) ebony fingerboard of the cello is mounted on the (typically) maple neck, and is where the strings are 'stopped' by the cellist to control their pitch when bowed or plucked. The fingerboard is gently concave along its length, with a very specific convex curve across its width.

3 SOUNDBOARD

The spruce top surface of the cello, also known as the 'belly', resonates in sympathy with the strings, which pass their vibrations to it through the bridge. The soundboard also transmits the vibrations to the maple back of the cello via the internal sound post and bass bar (not shown).

4 BODY

Together, the soundboard, back and the 'wall' between them, the ribs, make up the hourglass-shaped body of the cello. Comprising the upper bout, lower bout and waist, the body amplifies the vibrations of the strings via the bridge, and defines the tone of the instrument.

5 F-HOLES

The F-shaped cutouts on either side of the bridge serve two purposes: firstly, to help the soundboard to resonate freely, and secondly, to allow soundwaves to leave the violin, resulting in a louder sounding instrument.

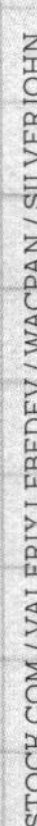

6 BRIDGE

The maple bridge provides the lower tension point for the vibrating section of the strings (the upper tension point being the nut, just below the pegs), and transmits string vibration to the soundboard, which resonates in sympathy. Below the bridge, inside the body, are the sound post and bass bar, which transmit the soundboard vibrations to the back of the cello.

7 TAILPIECE

This piece of wood at the bottom of the cello is where the strings are anchored. One or more fine-tuner screws are built into the tailpiece, allowing for more precise tensioning of the strings than is possible using the pegs alone.

8 TAIL SPIKE

This rod of metal is tipped with a sharp spike or rubber foot and locked in place by a thumb screw. The tail spike extends out of the body of the cello and is planted directly into the floor or a non-slip floor stop, to keep the cello in place and at the appropriate height for the player.

9 STRINGS

The four strings of the cello are generally tuned to perfect 5ths (from low to high: C, G, D and A); whereas those of the double bass are tuned in 4ths (from low to high: E, A, D and G). They're made of metal wound around a synthetic or metal core, or from the traditional 'catgut' (actually sheep intestine). Each type of string composition has its own characteristic sound.

10 BOW

The bow consists of a wooden shaft called the stick with a point at one end (the tip) and a brass nut at the other. A length of horsehair is tensioned between the tip and a wooden block (the frog) by the nut. Adjusting the nut moves the frog backwards or forwards, which increases or decreases the tension of the hair. When the bow is rubbed across the strings it causes them to vibrate, resonating the body of the cello/double bass via the bridge and generating sound. In order to promote friction, rosin (a resin derived from pines and other plants) needs to be regularly applied to the horsehair.

NOTATION GUIDE STRINGS

Notation for strings is written on the stave. Different instruments in the string family have different registers. The violin uses the treble (𝄞) clef, the viola uses the alto (𝄡) clef and the cello and double bass both use the bass (𝄢) clef. While the violin, viola and cello sound at the written pitch, the double bass sounds one octave lower than written. When arranging music for stringed instruments, it is common practice to divide the violins into two sections, called the 1st and 2nd violins. The standard format for a string quartet is two violins, a viola and a cello.

The ranges below are used in the Rockschool theory exams and are a good representation of the general ranges achievable by most musicians. As with other pitched instruments, more advanced players may be able to play higher notes than shown here. The double bass can also use a C attachment, which allows the player to extend their range by a third lower.

VIOLIN AND VIOLA

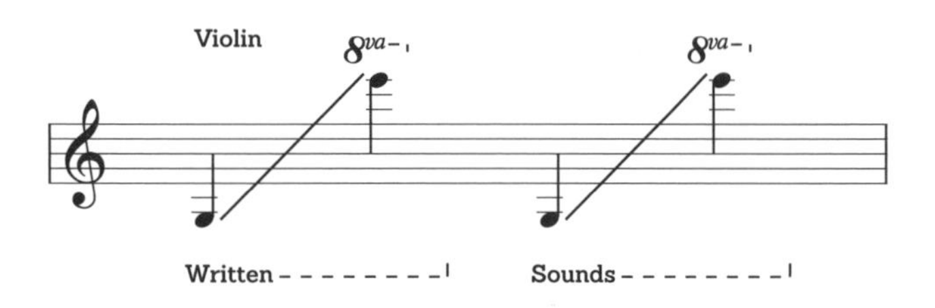

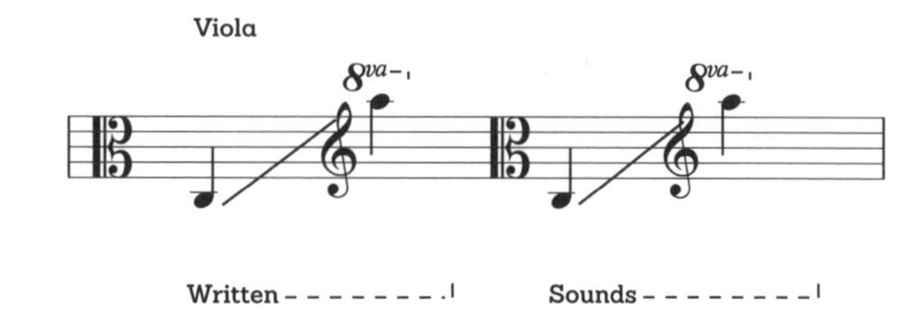

CELLO AND DOUBLE BASS

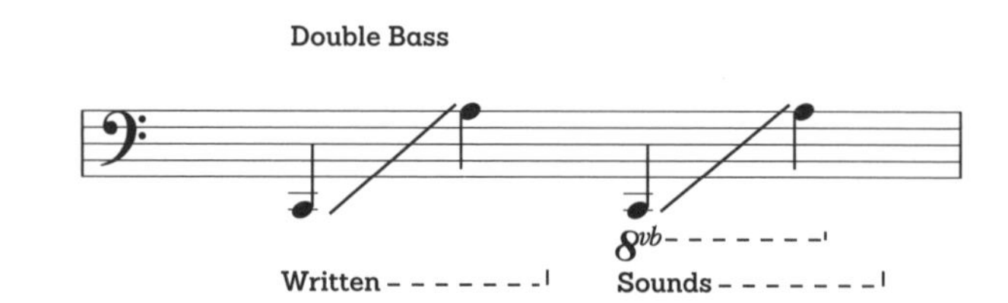

GRADE 8	NOTATION	DEFINITION
STACCATO		A staccato note is short and detached, signified by a dot above or below the notehead. It can be played with short up and down bow movements.
LEGATO		Legato is Italian for 'tied together', and means 'play smoothly'. This is shown with an arched line above or below a group of notes. To create the fluid effect, these notes are played in a single bow stroke.
ARCO	 *arco*	This simply means to play with the bow. This instruction is not necessary at the start of every piece of music to be played with the bow as arco is considered the 'default' performing method. However, if there is a section of pizzicato and the player is required to return to playing with the bow, then it is essential to add this instruction into the score.
PIZZICATO	 *pizz.*	Pizzicato (pizz.) means plucking the strings using fingers, but don't expect string players to play this technique as fast as a guitarist! This technique can create a light and open texture.
TREMOLANDO		A tremolando (also known as tremolo) on a stringed instrument can be played by moving the bow back and forth over a short distance very quickly, creating a wonderful shimmer effect. This is notated with three short diagonal lines drawn through the note stem. For whole notes, place the three lines above or below the notehead as appropriate.
SORDINO	 *con sord.*	A sordino (often notated as con sord., meaning with mute) is a mute that is placed over the bridge of a stringed instrument. It creates a muffled, dreamlike effect. This is particularly effective when the whole string section is muted together. To return to unmuted playing, it is important to add an instruction such as senza sordino (without mute).
PORTAMENTO	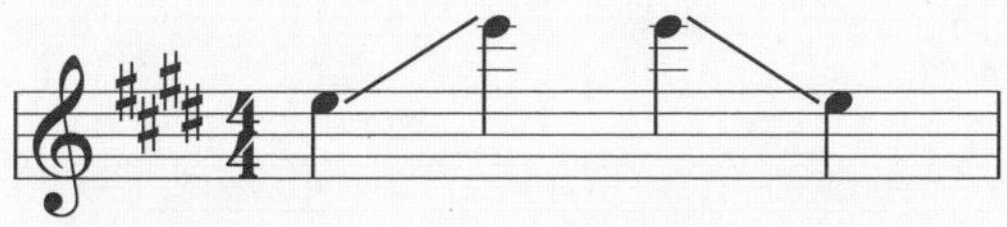	A portamento (sometimes called a glissando) is notated with a short line between two notes. The player slides from one pitch position on the fingerboard to the next without lifting the finger. A great example can be heard in the cello part of The Beatles' 'Strawberry Fields Forever'.

VARYING THE TONE

Many improving musicians, in their rush to gain speed and fluency on their instruments, neglect to work on a very different yet equally important musical skill: nurturing great tone. Yet to play or sing just one note and be instantly recognisable is a hallmark of the truly great musician. The first step along the road to achieving this goal is to understand the inner workings of the tools at your disposal – whether they're valves, cymbals, plug-ins or just your own body parts – and how they can influence the sound of your instrument, the way notes are formed and ultimately, your musical performance.

DRUMS

CYMBAL SIZES

The tone of individual cymbals can go some way to defining a drummer's sound. The choice is often dictated by the type of music being played. Smaller-diameter cymbals are higher in pitch and produce less volume and sustain; larger-diameter cymbals are lower in pitch and produce more volume and sustain. Thinner cymbals produce lighter tones; thicker cymbals are more durable.

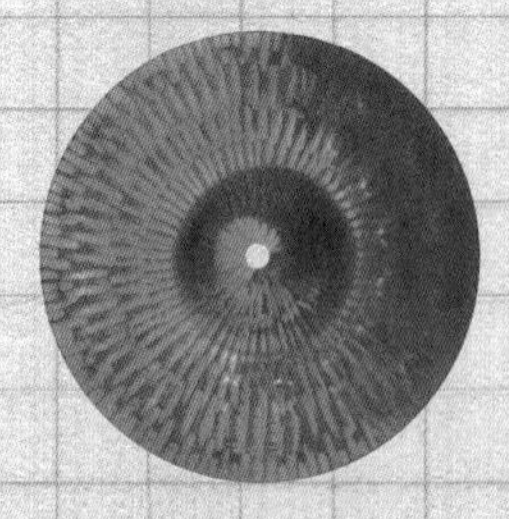

EFFECT CYMBALS

To expand their sonic palette further, drummers can add exotic-sounding china crash and splash cymbals to their kits. Of these 'effect' cymbals, the china is larger, heavier and plays with a denser, 'trashier' feel. The splash is smaller, and plays with a short, sharp crash sound.

VOCALS

TONAL VARIATIONS

SINGERS CAN alter the tone of their voice in many different ways, but because the techniques involve consciously modifying posture, breathing and anatomy – 'learned', habitual behaviours – learning them takes practice, and is often achieved through repetitive exercises. The two most common methods that are useful to know are performed using the tongue and the soft palate.

SOFT PALATE AND RAISING THE TONGUE

The soft palate is located just past the roof of the mouth, and is made of flexible muscle and cartilage. It is the area that moves up at the beginning of a yawn. Raising the back of the tongue and lowering the soft palate will create a more nasal tone.

FLATTENING THE TONGUE

Flattening the back of the tongue tends to open up the throat cavity, and will therefore produce a correspondingly more open, 'throaty' sound. Working on consciously controlling the tongue and soft palate is of great benefit to vocal tone.

KEYS

ACOUSTIC PIANO TONE

The strings on a grand piano are horizontal, with the hammer action moving up and down, assisted by gravity. The nature of this movement facilitates the player with fast action and note repetition when compared to the upright, which has vertical strings with the hammer action moving from side to side, assisted by springs. The longer keys on a grand piano also enable greater leverage, producing greater control, touch and harmonic content than on an upright.

ELECTRONIC PIANO TONE

Electronic pianos produce sound from recorded samples, so the quality of these samples affects the quality of the sound produced. There can be some limitations to electronic pianos/keyboards, including polyphony and natural effects such as reverb. However, many additional digital effects can be utilised and adapted, enabling the player to mix voices and create diverse sounds and tones.

GUITAR & BASS

PICKUP TYPES

THERE'S A seemingly endless variety of pickups for the electric guitarist and bassist to choose from nowadays, each promising different tonal variations based on the materials used in their construction. However, knowing the basics will help you to understand a lot about guitar tone.

SINGLE-COIL PICKUPS

Single-coil pickups are narrow pickups that you'll see fitted to many guitars, including classic models such as the Fender Stratocaster and Telecaster, and to basses such as the Fender Jazz Bass. Single coils produce a bright, cutting sound that's very versatile, though they can sound thin in heavier styles of rock music. The brighter tonality of single-coil pickups on a bass make them an ideal choice for fingerstyle playing, whereas split-coil pickups, such as those on a Fender Precision (consisting of two smaller pickups placed side by side, with each covering two strings) have a 'darker' tone than single coils, making them a popular choice for rock bassists.

HUMBUCKERS

Humbuckers contain two coils in one housing, and were originally designed to cancel out or 'buck' the hum produced by single-coil pickups. They produce a warm, mellow sound compared to single coils, and often have a higher output and more presence, making them ideally suited to rock styles. But because they tend to favour midrange frequencies, they can sound muddy in some situations. Most Gibson guitars, including the classic Les Paul model, are fitted with humbuckers. In the bass world, the Music Man StingRay is a classic example of a hard-hitting, humbucker-equipped bass.

SPECIALIST GEAR

All musicians rely on their equipment to some extent, and instrument manufacturers continually come up with new variations on their designs to suit trends and individual preferences. As musical genres evolve, new gear becomes available to suit the needs of players, and sometimes, innovative synthesisers, drum machines, guitar pedals and the like can even play a part in creating entirely new sub-genres based on the new sounds they offer.

Understanding how your equipment works, how to maintain it and how to use it to get the sounds you want is all part of the job of being a musician. Knowing more about your fellow musicians' equipment and how they use it will ultimately help you make music with them.

VOCALS

THERE ARE lots of different microphones, some specialised for recording particular instruments. Singers rely on two main types: dynamic and condenser.

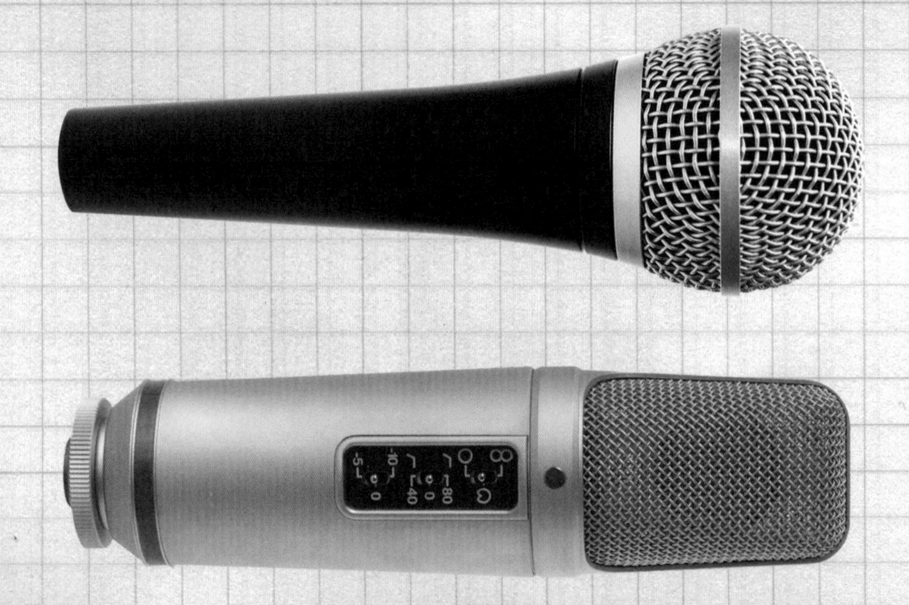

DYNAMIC MICS

Dynamic mics are usually used in live situations because they are robust, simpler in design than other types, can handle high volume levels and do not break easily. They are good for capturing loud instruments, but capture a smaller range of frequencies than condenser mics.

CONDENSER MICS

Condenser mics are very sensitive and capture a wider range of frequencies than dynamic microphones. They are also much more fragile than dynamic mics, and require a phantom power source; this, combined with their sensitivity to loud volumes, makes them much more suited to studio use than live use.

DRUMS

STICK THICKNESS

As well as being a matter of 'feel' for drummers, the thickness of the drum stick dictates weight, sound projection and durability. A thicker stick plays slower, with a heavier sound, and is more durable. A thinner stick plays faster, with a lighter sound, but is less durable.

STICK LENGTH

Stick length affects leverage – the force behind each hit – and has an impact on reach. A longer stick increases the leverage and power. A shorter stick plays with less, requiring the drummer to compensate.

TIPS

Tips generally give sticks greater durability and lifespan. Again, a tip with a smaller surface area plays with a lighter sound, with the benefit of adding clearer definition. Tips with a larger surface area play with a heavier feel.

KEYS

ACOUSTIC PIANO TYPES

Acoustic pianos fall into two main categories: the larger, deeper (often more expensive) grand piano, and the more commonly seen, smaller upright piano. As befits their name, grand pianos tend to have a fuller, richer, more balanced tone than upright pianos. This is a result of their larger size, longer strings and horizontal soundboard. Upright pianos typically have a slower action, and less touch control and responsiveness on account of their shorter keys. Also, the footpedals on a grand piano work in a more technical and sophisticated way than on an upright piano, and offer greater musicality.

ELECTRONIC PIANO TYPES

Modern electronic pianos are in effect synthesisers, which use layered samples of piano sounds to imitate an acoustic piano. These are not to be confused with the electric pianos developed in the mid-20th century, such as those made by Rhodes and Wurlitzer, which were actually electro-mechanical devices that converted struck or hammered string vibrations to electrical signals via pickups built into the instruments.

GUITAR & BASS

PLECTRUM TYPES

PLECTRUMS, OR picks, are made from a variety of different materials ranging from nylon to metal, and come in all shapes and sizes, with a variety of textures and grips. They can be loosely arranged into two groups: thin and thick.

THIN PICKS

Thin picks have a thin, bright sound, and are good for fast strumming, which makes them the preferred choice for many acoustic guitarists. Their flexibility means they lack a positive attack, which makes them less desirable for heavier styles of playing, or for styles that include a lot of single-note melody lines, although some bass players enjoy the 'soft-to-loud' dynamic range that using a thinner pick brings to their playing.

THICK PICKS

Thicker picks have a warm, full sound and a more immediate attack, which makes them suited to lead-guitar styles and bass playing. Their inflexibility can mean they snag in the strings when used for strumming and rhythm playing, and since most guitar players combine both approaches, a trade-off between clarity (thickness) and playability (flexibility) is usually reached.

EFFECTS

Compression, reverb, delay, distortion, modulation – effects are everywhere in modern music. In fact, certain types of effects are taken for granted so often that we no longer consciously realise we're listening to them. They've become part of the vocabulary of popular music. Because of this, it's vital that we learn to use effects authentically if we want to recreate specific musical styles, either live or during recording sessions.

Used sparingly, and with creativity, effects can elevate a recording or a performance to a higher level. Developing an understanding of the major effects types, and experimenting with them in your music, can lead to a wellspring of new musical ideas, and can help you find your own unique sound.

OVERDRIVE

This mild, crunchy distortion effect takes its name from the sound of a signal overdriving the valves of an amplifier. It's most commonly associated with guitar, but has also been used to great effect with harmonica, organ and even vocals. Its main role is to add sustain, warmth and bite to an instrument's sound.

HEAR IT ON **Cream** *Sunshine Of Your Love*, **The Strokes** *Last Nite* (vocals), **Oasis** *Cigarettes And Alcohol*

DISTORTION

Distortion is the aggressive, overpowering sound of rock and heavy metal guitar, which began with 1970s bands such as Led Zeppelin and Black Sabbath and evolved, in tandem with advances in technology, into the deafening thrash metal of Metallica, and the down-tuned roar of Mastodon.

HEAR IT ON **Metallica** *Enter Sandman*, **Avenged Sevenfold** *Bat Country*, **Bon Jovi** *You Give Love A Bad Name*

FUZZ

Fuzz sounds tinnier and less refined than other types of distortion. It sprang to prominence in the mid-1960s, powering the guitar sounds of Keith Richards, Jimi Hendrix and the psychedelic rock movement. Fuzz is also a popular way of dirtying up a bass sound.

HEAR IT ON **Jimi Hendrix Experience** *Purple Haze*, **The Rolling Stones** *(I Can't Get No) Satisfaction*, **The White Stripes** *Dead Leaves And The Dirty Ground*

COMPRESSION

Compression alters a sound by making the loudest parts quieter, and the quiet parts louder. Almost all recorded sounds have compression, and it is used in many creative ways – from adding attack and sustain to funk and country guitar, to smoothing vocal levels, to emphasising the pumping rhythms of electronic dance music.

HEAR IT ON **Pink Floyd** *Another Brick In The Wall, Part 2*, **Brad Paisley** *American Saturday Night*, **Adele** *Rolling In The Deep*

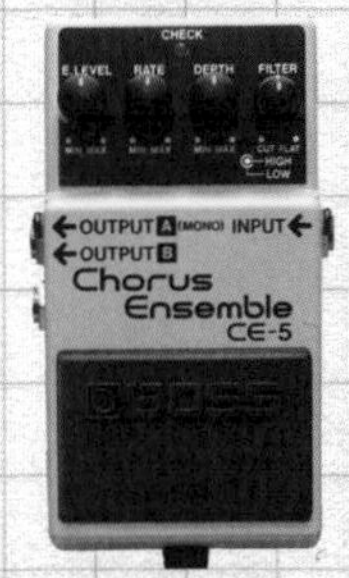

CHORUS

As the name suggests, chorus imitates the subtle variations in pitch that occur when the same part is being played or sung by two or more players at the same time (like a choir chorus). Mainly used in the 1980s on guitar, it is also associated with electric piano and synth.

HEAR IT ON **Prince** *Purple Rain*, **Guns N' Roses** *Paradise City*, **Nirvana** *Come As You Are*

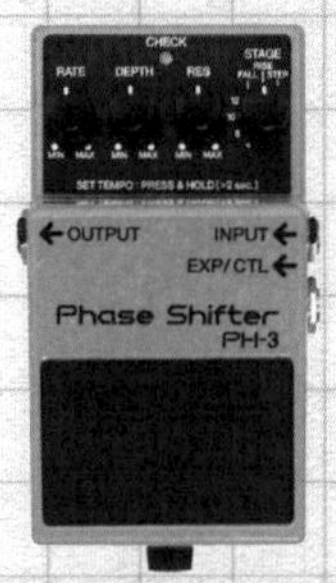

PHASER

Phase, like flange and chorus, is a 'modulation' effect – an effect in which the characteristic sound is achieved through one or more parameters being varied over time. Phasers provide a psychedelic 'sweeping' sound, the rate and intensity of which can be controlled, creating movement and texture in otherwise flat and static parts.

HEAR IT ON **The O'Jays** *For The Love Of Money*, **Queen** *One Vision*, **Blink-182** *Feeling This*

FLANGER

Taking its name from varying the speed of a reel-to-reel tape machine by running a finger along the 'flange', the flanger effect is a harmonically rich sweeping sound through high and low frequencies that is similar to but often more metallic than that of a phaser.

HEAR IT ON **The Cure** *A Forest*, **Lenny Kravitz** *Are You Gonna Go My Way*, **Van Halen** *Unchained*

DELAY

Delay is the repeating of a note or series of notes, either once or multiple times, at a set rate to create a rhythmic effect. It is used in all genres of music, from pop and rock to dub reggae and dance, and is a highly musical effect that can enhance all kinds of instruments, even drums and percussion.

HEAR IT ON **Pink Floyd** *Run Like Hell*, **U2** *Where The Streets Have No Name*, **The Police** *Walking On The Moon*

REVERB

Reverb, short for 'reverberation', is an effect that is used to imitate the way a sound naturally decays in a room. It creates a sense of depth and space in a mix of instruments, and can be applied to all sounds in ways ranging from natural and realistic to extreme and artificial-sounding.

HEAR IT ON **Dick Dale** *Misirlou*, **Chris Isaak** *Wicked Game*, **Jeff Buckley** *Hallelujah*

TREMOLO

Tremolo is one of the oldest effects. It was popularised by the US surf music craze of the 1960s and has been used by guitarists (and sometimes keyboard players) ever since. It works by varying the volume of a sound electronically at a pre-set rate, and sounds like an instrument is pulsing, throbbing or cutting in and out.

HEAR IT ON **Nancy Sinatra** *Bang Bang (My Baby Shot Me Down)*, **The Smiths** *How Soon Is Now*, **Black Keys** *Howlin' For You*

AUTO WAH/ENVELOPE FILTER

The auto wah, or envelope filter, works by emphasising certain frequencies while removing others from the signal of an instrument. Unlike a normal wah pedal, most auto wah/envelope filters respond to playing dynamics, so the effects are more obvious when the instrument is played more aggressively, such as when playing slap bass.

HEAR IT ON **Stevie Wonder** *Higher Ground*, **Red Hot Chili Peppers** *Falling Into Grace*, **Edie Brickell & New Bohemians** *What I Am*

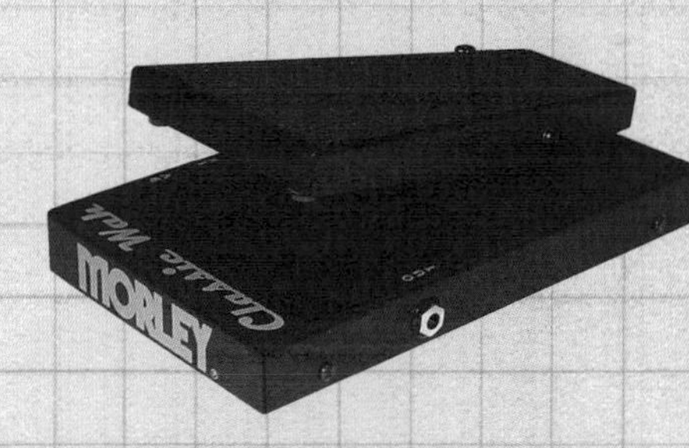

WAH

Wah is named after the vocal-like sound it creates. On a guitar, a wah-pedal effect moves a frequency peak in response to the position of the pedal, making the part played sound like someone singing "wah wah". The rhythmic possibilities of wah have been explored by guitarists in funk, blues, rock and many other genres besides.

HEAR IT ON **The Jimi Hendrix Experience** *Voodoo Child (Slight Return)*, **Funkadelic** *Maggot Brain*, **U2** *The Fly*

BAND ANALYSIS

The Band Analysis section of the exam draws on all the individual elements of music you have studied so far, such as music notation, harmony, scales, transposition and instrument knowledge, and puts them into a band context in the form of a multi-instrument score. In Grades 6–8, four new genres (country, jazz, soul and reggae) are added to those covered in the earlier grades (rock, pop, blues, metal and funk). The scores also feature a wider range of instruments, with horns and strings being added alongside the more conventional band instruments.

The following pages discuss the music genres relevant to Band Analysis, and identify some of the common building blocks of popular music style, referred to as "musical devices" in the exam. The musical devices represent the type of material you can cite if asked to identify style references and influences in the scores.

Each of the styles presented concludes with a brief selection of recommended listening, which should be followed up with further research of your own into the sounds, bands, instruments and techniques that typify the genre.

ROCK

The Rolling Stones have been a dominant force in rock music for over half a century

Rock music evolved out of 1950s rock 'n' roll. In the 1960s, rock musicians took rock 'n' roll's basic instrumentation, energy and showmanship as a starting point before expanding on its rigid blues-based formula, adding new sounds, extending song structures, tackling more complex lyrical themes and increasing the boundaries of technical virtuosity. By the 1970s, distinct musical subgenres had emerged; even today, rock continues to incorporate sounds and musical ideas from other styles into its vocabulary. At the forefront of mainstream music for over half a century, rock has been used as a vehicle for counter-cultural and political movements, from Woodstock and the Vietnam War to punk and Live Aid. The electric guitar is rock's dominant instrument, and the guitar riff remains the genre's signature, along with 4/4 meter and the verse-chorus song structures inherited from earlier musical forms. Rock's core instruments are guitar, electric bass, drums and vocals. Its most common formats are the power trio, the quartet and the five-piece (however, acts can vary in size from solo artists all the way up to the likes of 20-piece ensemble, The Polyphonic Spree). Sub-genres such as blues rock, prog rock, jazz rock and New Wave introduced keys and synths, while instruments from the classical and traditional worlds have also been used.

COMMON ROCK PROGRESSIONS

ROCK CHORD progressions can often be very simple and most rock songs stay in a single musical key throughout. The first example here shows a widely used 'chord loop' where chords I, V, VIm and IV of the home key (in this case C major) are played over and over in whole bar or half-bar changes. The second example is a modal chord progression in E Mixolydian. The Roman numerals show the chord numbers in relation to the key signature.

4/4 ‖: C / / / | G / / / | Am / / / | F / / / :‖
I V VIm IV

4/4 ‖: E / / / | A / / / | E / D / | E / / / :‖
I IV I ♭VII I

BASS PART IN ROOT POSITION

THE ELECTRIC bass in a rock band typically plays the root of the chord, creating texture and power in the low end of the mix. In this example the bass is following the guitar chords in root position until bar 3, where it briefly plays an F♯ note, putting the guitar part's D chord in its first inversion.

GUITAR RIFFS WITH OPEN STRINGS

MANY ROCK songs are based around the riff (usually a repeated rhythmic and melodic phrase). As many are written on electric guitar, rock players have taken advantage of the resonant open strings available in rock's go-to keys of E and A (and E and A minor) to create memorable, catchy-sounding figures.

GUITAR RIFFS WITH MOVING POWERCHORDS

IT'S POSSIBLE to combine chord progressions and melodies by moving a powerchord. Riffs featuring these moving powerchord riffs are usually one, two or four bars in length. This example is in the key of C minor.

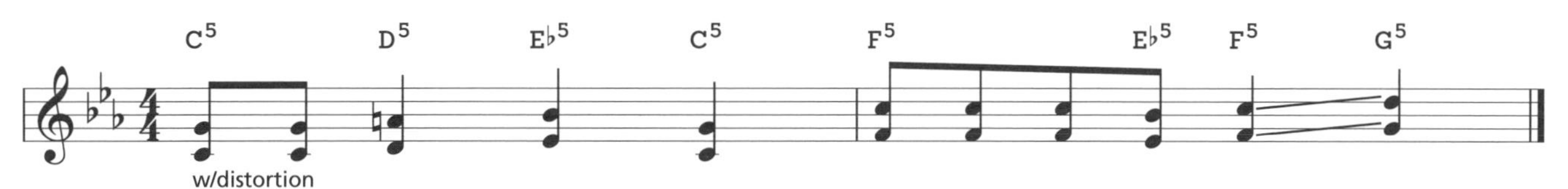

POP

Michael Jackson was the ultimate pop singer, songwriter, performer and star

What is meant by 'pop'? Even if you define it as 'music made for mass commercial appeal', that still leaves you with artists as diverse as The Beatles and Jay-Z. Common to most pop is a song length of around three minutes, as a result of songs traditionally being written for radio and the single format. Pop also has formulaic song structures designed to be familiar on first listen, while vocal melodies, musical hooks and choruses target the listener's attention. Pop balances its relatively unsophisticated musicianship with cutting-edge production techniques. In doing so it incorporates musical ideas from various genres, but tends to present them in a more commercial way. Pop isn't defined by one type of musical lineup, but it is dominated by one type of musician: the vocalist. Melodic vocal performance is paramount to a pop record's success, and where blues, rock 'n' roll and jazz tend to be male-dominated, pop is an equal-opportunity employer, especially where singers are concerned. Pop has always borrowed from underground music, and pop from each decade is characterised by a specific style, such as synth pop in the 1980s, dance music in the 1990s, hip hop in the 2000s, and electronica and R&B in the 2010s.

POP CHORD PROGRESSIONS

THESE CHORD progressions are examples of four-chord loops. Some pop songs consist of the same chord loop played throughout; others vary the chords in different parts of the song.

4/4 ||: C / / / | G / / / | Am / / / | F / / / :||
I | V | VIm | IV

4/4 ||: Em / / / | C / / / | G / / / | D / / / :||
Im | ♭VI | ♭III | ♭VII

POP BASSLINES

IN POP, the bass functions as part of the rhythm section, often working with the bass drum to create a danceable feel. Pop basslines are typically simple, harmonically and rhythmically, although sometimes the bass can underpin the whole track with its own repeating riff.

VOCAL HARMONIES

VOCAL HARMONIES are an evergreen feature of pop, particularly in eras where vocal ensembles have dominated. The backing vocals (BVs) can follow the words sung by the main vocal to create texture (typically in a chorus) or can have their own separate 'call and response' part, responding to the main vocal.

POP DRUMS WITH PERCUSSION

MAINSTREAM POP is designed to appeal to large numbers of people and so 4/4 pop drumbeats are often 'danceable', typically placing a solid bass-drum emphasis on the downbeat and with a consistent snare on the second and fourth beats. Sub-beats can be filled with more rhythmically complex material, and pop drum-kit parts are often augmented with percussion such as shakers, tambourine, cabasa or claves.

BLUES

B.B. King, the undisputed King of the blues

Blues developed from the musical traditions of slaves brought to America in the 19th Century, and its call-and-response structure and cyclical 12-bar, I-IV-V format derive from these early spiritual and worksong forms. So-called because of the melodic targeting of 'blue' notes (the flattened 3rd, 5th and 7th of the major scale), much of blues's identity lies in its ambiguity between major and minor tonality. The ability of the guitar and harmonica to 'bend' notes to add subtle microtonal nuances made for highly individualistic soloing styles, and the use of a slide on the strings of a guitar tuned to an open chord enabled players to mimic the wailing of a human voice. Blues can be played without any accompaniment, as a solo vocalist accompanied by guitar or piano, or in a range of formats that often expand to include harmonica, backing vocalists, piano, keys and horn sections. The guitar's centrality to the blues and its wealth of opportunity for expressive soloing has resulted in an unending stream of blues-guitar heroes taking the spotlight, but the genre has seen its fair share of non-six-string virtuosos, too, such as harmonica players Little Walter and Junior Wells, and pianist Otis Spann.

CLASSIC 12-BAR PROGRESSION

THE CHORD chart below shows the basic structure of the 12-bar blues. There are many variations, and the two bracketed chords show one way in which musicians often vary that structure to add colour and movement to the form. The final two bars often contain a melodic fragment called a 'turnaround'.

Bar	1	2	3	4	5	6
4/4 𝄆	D^7 / / /	(G^7) / / /	D^7 / / /	/ / / /	G^7 / / /	/ / / /
	I^7	(IV^7)	I^7		IV^7	

Bar	7	8	9	10	11	12
	D^7 / / /	/ / / /	A^7 / / /	G^7 / / /	D^7 / / /	(A^7) / / / 𝄇
	I^7		V^7	IV^7	I^7	(V^7)

24-BAR BLUES PROGRESSION

IT'S POSSIBLE to play a 24-bar blues simply by doubling the number of measures per chord. This is more common at higher tempos.

SHUFFLE AND STRAIGHT RHYTHMS

BLUES TRACKS are often performed with a shuffle/swung rhythm, where every other eighth note is shorter than the previous one. This is also known as a broken triplet feel and can be notated by inserting ♫ = ♩ ♪ at the top of the score and then writing all the subsequent eighth notes normally. If the broken triplet feel of the music is particularly slow, an alternative method is to notate the whole track in 12/8 time, and then notate each broken triplet as it is heard. These examples would be heard as exactly the same notes/rhythms but performed at different tempos.

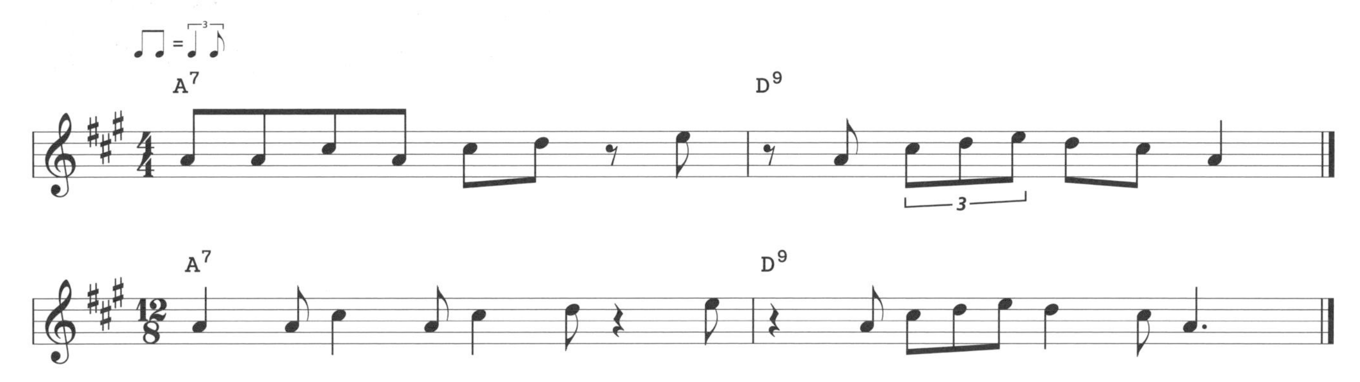

MINOR AND MAJOR BLUES

BLUES MELODIES can be minor or major. In either case, the seventh note of the scale is almost always minor ('flattened'). It's also possible to play melodies with a minor 3rd even when the underlying chord is major, sometimes raising the minor 3rd note very slightly sharp – this is known as a blue note. Blue notes can be notated as quarter tones, as shown here, or simply written as minor intervals and left to the player's discretion.

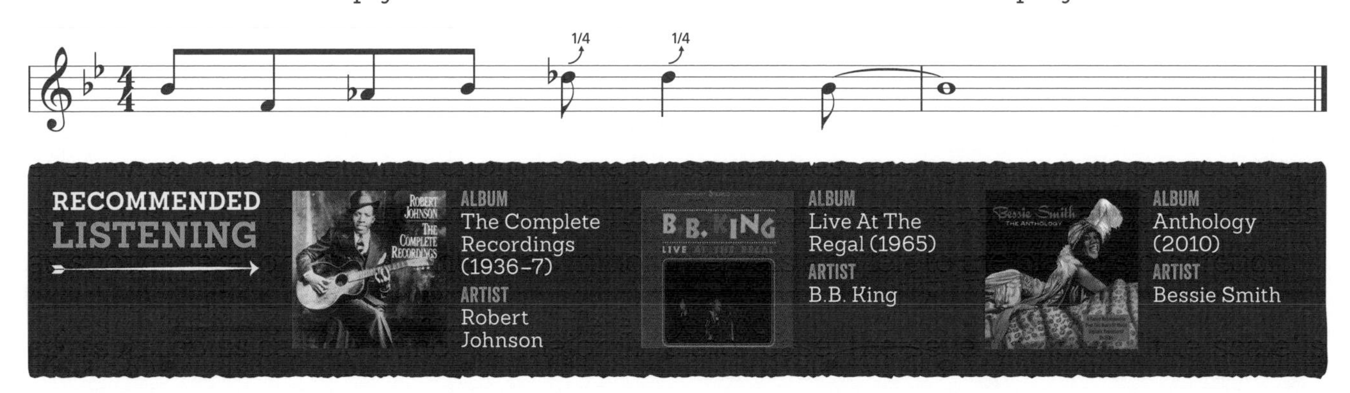

METAL

Black Sabbath's Tony Iommi, the original Dark Lord of heavy-metal riffery

As rock groups of the late 1960s such as Led Zeppelin and Black Sabbath began touring stadiums and demanding ever-louder gear, metal was forged. These groups presented a powerchord-driven take on rock's blues-inspired riffs, insistent drums and virtuoso soloing and bound it to darker lyrical themes. The subsequent development of metal was like an arms race, with the emphasis increasingly placed on speedy guitar playing, double bass-drum pedal kits, galloping basslines and operatic vocal ranges. In the 1980s, thrash metal bands such as Megadeth, Metallica and Slayer were the next logical progression. Meanwhile, virtuoso 'shred' guitarists expanded the vocabulary of the lead guitar, often incorporating neo-classical instrumental influences. Countless sub-genres arose in the decades that followed. The classic line-up of vocals, bass, drums and twin guitarists is sometimes augmented by keys players, but in the main the lead guitarists occupy the limelight. Metal guitar has produced all kinds of technical innovations, from the two-handed tapping of Eddie Van Halen all the way to the current trend for downtuned rhythms with seven- and eight-string instruments, and a focus on rhythmic sophistication and intricate time signatures.

METAL RHYTHM GUITAR

METAL GUITAR'S greatest exponents aren't all lead guitar players. Rhythm guitar styles have changed significantly over the years, and it's from these changes that many sub-genres of metal have emerged. Whatever the particular genre, metal rhythm playing is a highly demanding skill that involves precision, stamina and an ability to dampen strings to control the extraneous noise created by a distorted guitar at ear-splitting volumes.

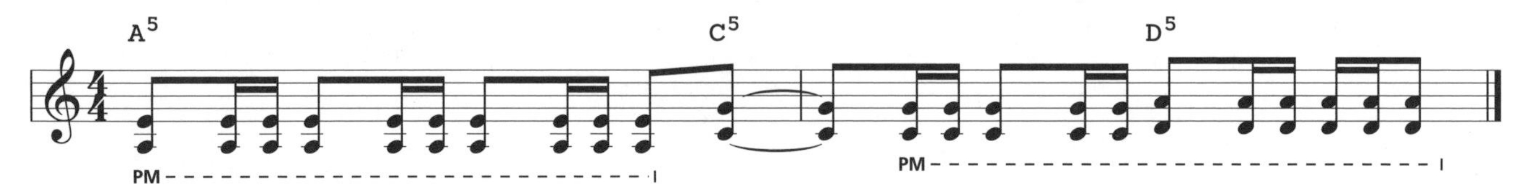

METAL CHORD PROGRESSIONS

METAL IS rarely performed in a major key and frequently uses chromatic intervals and non-diatonic or modal progressions. This example uses powerchords in the home key of E minor; chords of F5 and B♭5 provide a ♭2 and ♭5 interval, as used in many metal sub-genres to create dissonance.

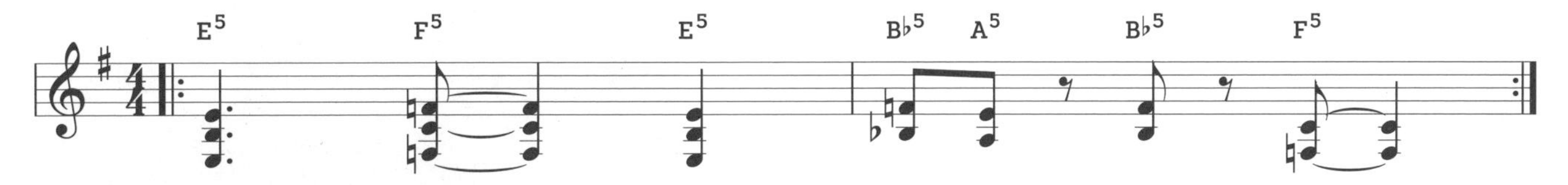

TWO-HANDED TAPPING

EDDIE VAN Halen opened up new possibilities for rock guitar when he debuted his fluid tapping style on his 1978 instrumental, 'Eruption'. Tapping consists of using the fingers of both hands to perform a rapid sequence of hammer-ons and pull-offs on the same string to produce lightning-fast arpeggios impossible to play any other way.

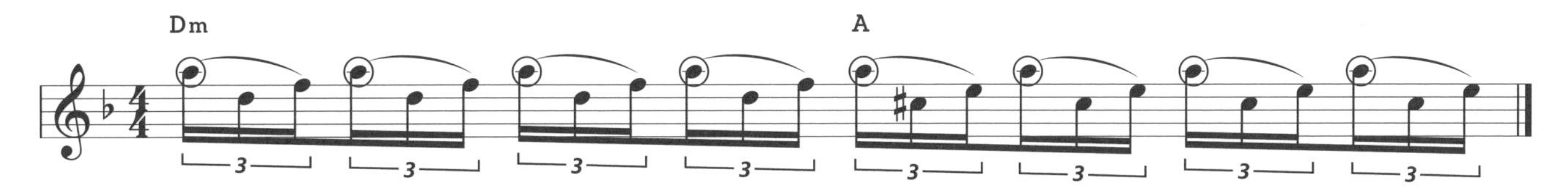

BASS PEDAL NOTES

BECAUSE METAL relies on power and energy more than rapid harmonic changes, one common musical device is the pedal note, where the bass plays the same note throughout, while the guitars change chords. In this example, the first two bars feature a pedal note, leading into a unison riff in bars 3 and 4.

RECOMMENDED LISTENING

ALBUM
Black Sabbath (1970)
ARTIST
Black Sabbath

ALBUM
The Number Of The Beast (1982)
ARTIST
Iron Maiden

ALBUM
Master Of Puppets (1986)
ARTIST
Metallica

JAZZ

Miles Davis is widely acknowledged as one of the most influential figures in jazz history

The term jazz covers a multitude of sub-genres. Some, such as dixieland and swing, are simpler and more diatonically based. Others, such as bebop, cool and modal jazz, tend to be more harmonically sophisticated, making more use of extended and altered chords, and modes. Many jazz chord sequences revolve around the chords II, V and I rather than the I, IV and V so typical of pop. They are also likely to make more use of chords built upon the second, third and seventh degrees of the major scale. Jazz has remained popular since its evolution from blues, ragtime and other styles in the late 19th century. Part of its enduring appeal can be attributed to jazz musicians absorbing other styles of music, creating endless fusions, such as jazz blues, Latin jazz and jazz funk. While jazz is often played solo (e.g. piano), it is also played in a variety of instrumental combinations, from duos to Big Bands. A typical sextet might comprise piano, double bass, drums, trumpet, alto sax and electric guitar. However, all kinds of skilled instrumentalists have achieved popularity in jazz, such as the acoustic guitarist Django Reinhardt and the harmonica player Toots Thielemans.

DIATONIC CHORDS

THIS CHORD sequence shows a simple extract of 'rhythm changes', a progression named after Gershwin's 'I've Got Rhythm'. As you loop back round from the repeat you complete the chord progression IIm V I, which forms the backbone of many jazz standards such as 'Autumn Leaves', 'Perdido' and 'Giant Steps'.

4/4 ||: C / Am / | Dm / G / :||

I VIm IIm V

EXTENDED CHORDS AND ALTERED CHORDS

THIS PROGRESSION is much more harmonically challenging. It uses extended chords (the A♭13 and Cmaj7) and altered chords (such as the A7♯5). The B♭7♭5 and A♭13 chords are rooted on notes not found within the home key, however, they are chromatic passing chords, adding complex tensions and resolutions to the underlying chord sequence. Don't worry, you're not expected to analyse scores to this depth, but it is worth becoming familiar with both the sound and look of jazz harmony.

4/4	B♭7♭5	A7♯5	A♭13	G7♭9	Cmaj7	E7♯5♯9
		VI		V	I	III

CHROMATIC WALKING BASS

OTHER STYLES of music, such as rockabilly, rock 'n' roll and blues, all make heavy use of the walking bassline, but jazz adds its own slant by approaching the main chord tones from a note a semitone above or below. This example demonstrates the technique over the 'rhythm changes' progression shown previously.

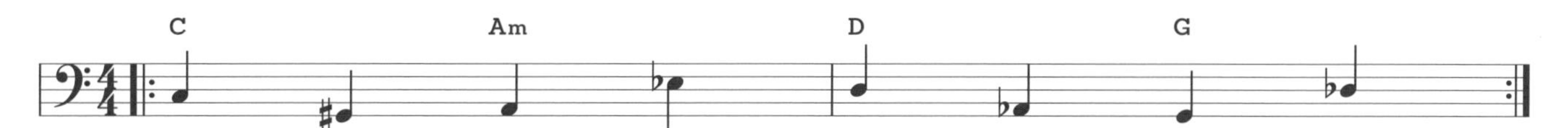

SWING RIDE PATTERNS

RIDE AND hi-hat parts featuring a repeated pattern of a quarter note followed by a pair of swung eighth notes are common, appearing on recordings such as 'Straight, No Chaser' (Thelonious Monk), 'Take Five' (Dave Brubeck) and 'Milestones' (Miles Davis).

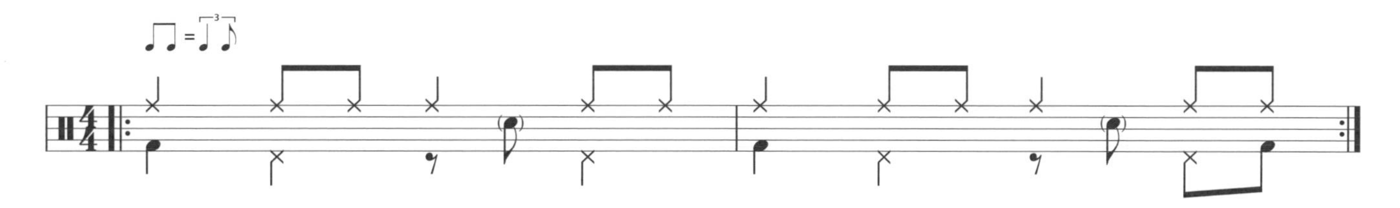

SOUL

Aretha Franklin's powerful gospel-style vocal delivery established her as the Queen of Soul

Soul is an umbrella term for a diverse range of African-American music with common influences from gospel and R&B. Its distinct flavours are referred to either by the regions of the US they were created in or after the record labels that masterminded the style's rise to prominence, such as Stax and Motown. Gospel's call and response vocals, ensemble singing and approach to chord substitutions and progressions are common to most soul music, but where Detroit-based Motown took these in a pop direction, southern acts had a harder, more emotionally raw sound. Soul was often created by session musicians, and featured innovative recording techniques and sometimes lavish arrangements. Horns, strings, piano and keys were added to a core of bass, drums, percussion and guitar. Some of the most respected bands of all time worked in the genre, arranging and recording hit after hit in a pressurised, almost factory-like environment. Stax had Booker T. & The M.G.'s, Motown had the Funk Brothers, and while each act may have been marketed on the strength of its vocalists, it was the behind-the-scenes work of these creative and disciplined musicians that fuelled soul's engine rooms.

DIATONIC SOUL CHORD PROGRESSIONS

SOUL PROGRESSIONS are often harmonically simple, typically based on diatonic chords and staying within the home key throughout. The chord suffixes can sometimes be extended by equivalent 9, 11 and 13 chords. In this example, the I-IIIm-IV-V loop is notated in a 1960s soul style as diatonic 7 chords, which are extended in bar 3 and 4 to provide a more sophisticated version of the same underlying chord loop.

4/4	Bar 1		Bar 2		Bar 3		Bar 4	
Chord	$Gmaj^7$ /	Bm^7 /	$Cmaj^7$ /	D^7 /	$Gmaj^9$ /	Bm^9 /	$Cmaj^9$ /	D^{13} /
Function	$I maj^7$	$III m^7$	$IV maj^7$	V^7	$I maj^9$	$III m^9$	$IV maj^9$	V^{13}

STEVE CROPPER-STYLE GUITAR LICKS

THE HORN players that Stax guitarist Steve Cropper was surrounded by must have made an impression on him. The guitar figures he played on countless hits, with their sliding chords, three-string shapes and licks built from harmonised 6ths, could almost be imitations of ensemble horns.

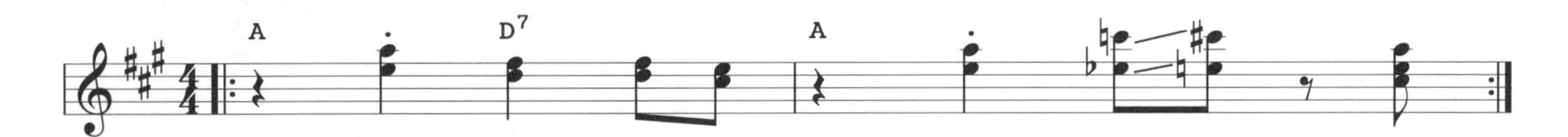

JAMES JAMERSON-STYLE MELODIC BASSLINE

JAMES JAMERSON played bass on more than 30 number-one records, and Motown's much-praised grooves owe him a huge debt. This typical Jamerson-style riff is based on a major pentatonic scale, using the root, 5th and 6th of the underlying major chords.

UP-TEMPO SOUL DRUM PATTERNS

IN FASTER soul tracks, and particularly in some 1960s Motown and Stax, the bass drum can play a part in adding propulsion to the groove, doubling some of the hi-hat's eighth notes. This example is based on the well-used pattern that appears in Wilson Pickett's 'Midnight Hour' and Aretha Franklin's 'Respect'.

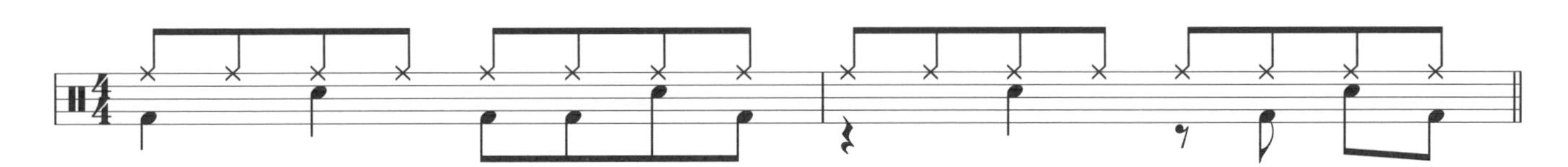

FUNK

Parliament and Funkadelic supremo George Clinton

James Brown may have been the Godfather of Soul, but he was also the Father of Funk. In the late 1960s, songs like 'Cold Sweat' emphasised the first beat of the bar and sported roving basslines, percussive guitar and horn parts woven around a vocal. By the 1970s, acts like Sly And The Family Stone and Parliament/Funkadelic (P-Funk) developed Brown's sound. Funk is characterised by its lack of chord changes; instead, the extended chords of bebop feature over extended, single-chord jams. Plenty of genres have co-opted the techniques of funk, most notably disco and, to a lesser extent, jazz. In the 1980s, funk returned in updated guise via the likes of Prince and Red Hot Chili Peppers. The stripped-back, rhythmic style of classic funk can be achieved with bass, drums and guitar, but it's at its best when supplemented by keys and a brass section, typically consisting of saxophone, trumpet and trombone. More modern, 1980s funk-influenced music replaced the horns with synths. Funk has its fair share of virtuoso soloists, such as guitarists Eddie Hazel and Ernie Isley. But don't forget the all-important rhythm section, with drummers such as Joseph 'Zigaboo' Modeliste and bass players like Bootsy Collins among funk's greats.

EXTENDED CHORDS

FUNK OFTEN makes use of extended chords, where notes beyond the octave are added to underlying 7 chords (e.g. major 7s, minor 7s, dominant 7s) to create more advanced harmony. The essence of funk is the combination of extended harmony and rhythmic sophistication. In this example, this major-key progression is extended so that the chords are all major 9s, dominant 9s or dominant 11s.

4/4 ||: $Gmaj^9$ / / / | $Cmaj^9$ / D^9 / | $Gmaj^9$ / / / | $Cmaj^9$ / D^{11} / :||

$Imaj^9$ | $IVmaj^9$ V^9 | $Imaj^9$ | $IVmaj^9$ V^{11}

HORN PART

IN FUNK bands, the core rhythm section – typically drums, electric bass, guitar and keyboards – can be augmented with additional instrumentation including percussion, backing vocals and horns. The horn part shown here would typically be played as an accompaniment under a vocal part, because it features staccato 'stabs' in time with the snare drum.

FUNK-STYLE RHYTHM GUITAR

THE GUITAR'S rhythmic possibilities were taken to extremes with the pioneering players of the funk movement. Palm muting, extended chords, fast changes through three-string triads and metronomic right-hand rhythmic control are all key to a great funk part.

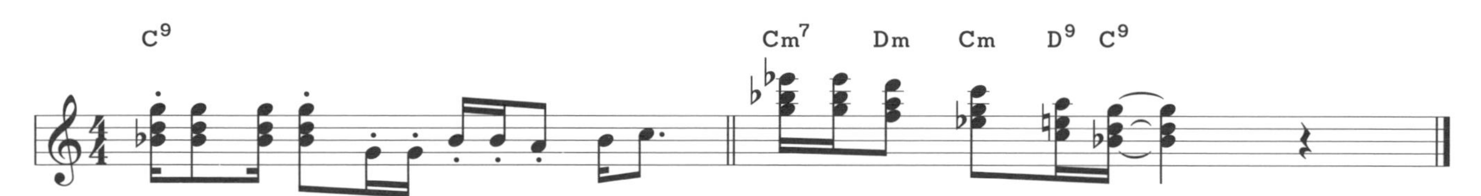

FUNK DRUM PART WITH SNARE DISPLACEMENT

MOST FUNK tracks are based around a 16th-note groove. This allows for substantial syncopation. In this example, the snare and bass drum are displaced so that they place emphasis on weaker beats of the bar, creating rhythmic interest and establishing, through repetition of the pattern, a funky groove.

COUNTRY

Dolly Parton is one of country music's most prolific artists, having written over 3000 songs

Country originated in the south of the USA in the 1920s, a blend of the styles that preceded it containing influences from cowboy songs, gospel, blues and European folk. Country is often characterised by eight-bar song structures and title-based choruses that encourage community singing. Like many folk music styles, country makes extensive use of (particularly major) pentatonic scales in its melodies, sometimes with a chromatic passing note. Songs are often harmonically diatonic, sometimes using only the basic I, IIm, IIIm, IV, V and VIm triads, and progressions typically begin and end on the home key chord. Country songs usually feature a chorus, although there are some written in AABA form (verse-verse-bridge-verse), notably Willie Nelson's 'You Are Always On My Mind' and Hank Williams Jr's 'Your Cheatin' Heart'. Because country grew out of American folk music, its roots are in portable stringed instruments, particularly the acoustic guitar. Country bands rely on high-quality musicianship, and virtuoso solos (typically violin, mandolin, guitar or banjo) are common. Country lyrics often deal with themes of home, love, commitment and rural life, and the simple harmony underscores core ideas of sincerity, nostalgia and loyalty.

TYPICAL COUNTRY PROGRESSIONS

ALL OF these progressions are examples of simple country harmony in a major key. The changes are all diatonic and the chords are not extended beyond the octave.

4/4

G / / /	C / / /	G / / /	D / / /	G / / /	C / / /	G / D /	G / / /
I	IV	I	V	I	IV	I V	I

4/4

G / D /	Em / / /	C / / /	D / / /	Em / D /	C / G /	C / D /	G / / /
I V	VIm	IV	V	VIm V	IV I	IV V	I

FIDDLE DOUBLESTOPS WITH TELECASTER-STYLE LICKS

THE GUITAR features prominently in country music. Acoustic guitars have long been used for accompaniment by singer/songwriters, while electric guitars are a staple of the country band. Some of the signature sounds of country guitar are actually imitations of other instruments. Players such as Jerry Donahue and Albert lee helped to popularise double stopping techniques reminiscent of fiddle playing, along with elaborate string bending influenced by the sound of the steel guitar.

BASS SIMPLICITY

THE ROLE of the bass in country music is to underpin the harmony, and it often does this as simply as possible. This classic country root-fifth bassline follows the chords harmonically, and rhythmically does not deviate from the first and third beats of the bar.

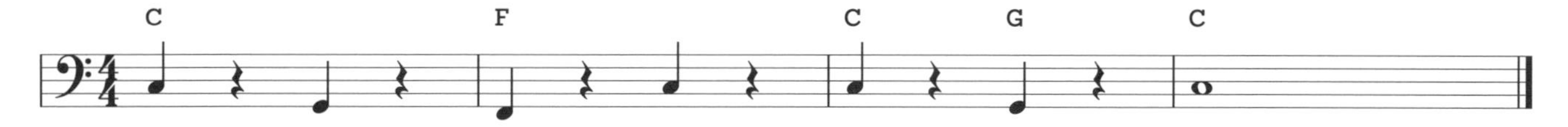

COUNTRY SCALE

THE SO-CALLED 'country scale' is a modal inversion of the blues scale, and consists of all of the notes of the major pentatonic scale with the addition of a minor 3rd. Typically the minor 3rd is used as a chromatic passing note, immediately followed by the major 3rd. The scale can be used by any melodic instrument when improvising in a major key.

REGGAE

Reggae's iconic superstar, the late Bob Marley

© IAN DICKSON / REX

Reggae emerged in Jamaica in the 1960s as a development of ska and rocksteady. Whereas ska is characterised by its uptempo, danceable sound and strict quarter-note walking basslines, reggae is played at a more languid tempo, and has a more melodic and rhythmically varied approach to its basslines. The famous 'skank' rhythm (single or double upstroke of guitar on the offbeat) became a hallmark. Reggae is strictly 4/4 in meter, and uses relatively straightforward chord structures; the interplay between vocals and instrumental parts is often based on the call-and-response formula. Reggae's global influence can be heard in 2 Tone, hip hop, rock and even punk, as well as in direct offshoots such as dub, dancehall and ragga. The principal instruments of reggae are drums, bass and guitar, with supporting roles from horn sections and piano and keys. The stripped-down discipline of reggae's drum patterns and simple chord structures enable a syncopated, wandering style of bass playing. Reggae also has its own drum patterns, known as one drops, rockers and steppers. Horn sections play counter melodies in unison, and typically comprise sax, trumpet and trombone.

TYPICAL MAJOR-KEY REGGAE CHORD PROGRESSIONS

IN MANY classic reggae tracks the chords used are all straightforward diatonic triads in root position, and are rarely extended to 7s or 9s. These examples are all based on chords I, IV and V, and are shown here in the key of A major. Because reggae is syncopated music, the listener is engaged through texture and groove rather than harmonic sophistication.

4/4 A / / /	/ / / /	/ / / /	/ / / /	D / / /	/ / / /	/ / / /	/ / / /	
I				IV			

4/4 A / / /	/ / / /	D / / /	E / / /	A / / /	/ / / /	D / / /	E / / /	
I		IV	V	I		IV	V

THE 'SKANK'

THIS RHYTHM guitar technique involves strumming a brief percussive chord on beats two and four, which is silenced by damping the strings, usually with the fretting hand. Chords are often partial chords on the treble strings, and the technique usually employs an upstroke to avoid unwanted sound from the lower strings. In this example, bars 1 and 2 feature a slow reggae skank on beats two and four; bars 3 and 4 show a double-speed eighth-note skank, which is more typical of reggae's precursor, ska.

REGGAE EIGHTH-NOTE BASSLINES

REGGAE'S POWER often comes from avoiding the downbeat. This typical bassline is based on the root, 5th and 6th of the chord, and can be moved with the harmony. It is shown here played as eighth notes followed by the same notes as 16ths (double speed). These basslines sound different in context because they have a different relationship to the second and fourth beats of the bar, where the off-beat skank would be played.

DRUM PARTS WITH SPACE

BASS DRUM placement in the bar is used to define the beat for dancers. Below are three different approaches. The bass drum begins by playing beats two and four (known as a 'one drop'), followed by beats one and three (a 'rocker'), and finally by playing on all four beats (a 'stepper').

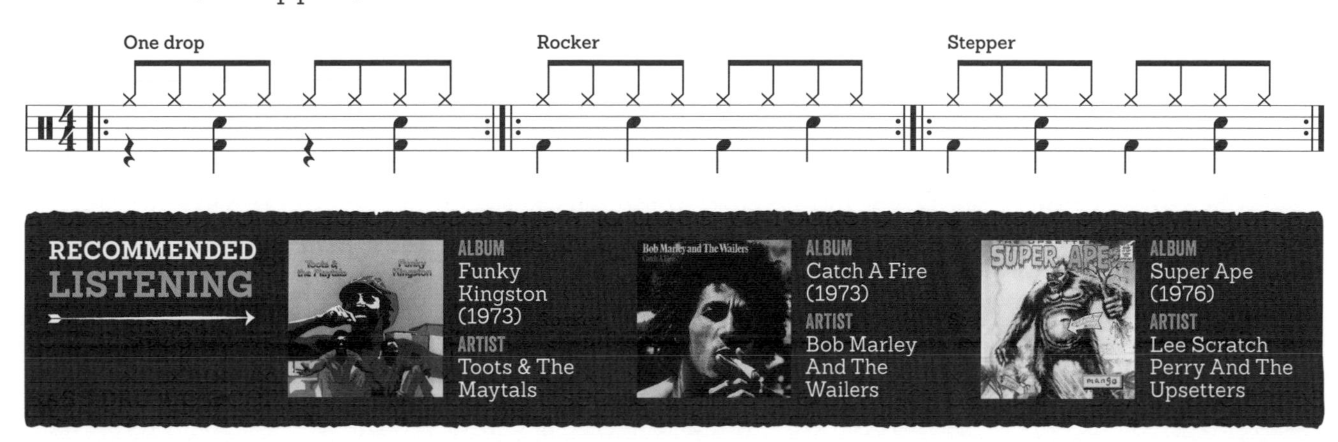

USEFUL INFORMATION

The language of music is an international language and, like all language, it is constantly evolving and subject to many regional variations. Whilst creating a comprehensive list of every musical term and its variants is beyond the intention of this book, Rockschool have compiled a list of common terms and symbols which are often subject to variations that you may come across in a contemporary music setting.

CHORDS

Chord symbol notation is often the subject of much discussion and personal preference. The information below is a table showing some of the various options you may encounter, but certain symbols may NOT be what we believe to be the most effective way of relaying information and as such, the Rockschool graded exam questions will only contain the symbols and terminology referred to previously in Books 1 and 2.

The key of C is used for illustrative purposes

TRIADS		
C major	C, Cmaj, CM	1,3,5
C minor	Cm, Cmin, C-	1,♭3,5
C diminished	Cdim, C°	1,♭3,♭5
C augmented	Caug, C+	1,3,♯5
C suspended 4	Csus4	1,4,5
C suspended 2	Csus2	1,2,5

SEVENTH CHORDS: 4 PART		
C major 7	Cmaj7, C△7, C△	1,3,5,7
C minor 7	Cm7, Cmin7, C-7	1,♭3,5,♭7
C dominant 7	C7, Cdom7	1,3,5,♭7
C dominant 7 sus 4	C7sus4, Cdom7 sus4	1,4,5,♭7
C dominant7♯5	C7♯5, Cdom7♯5, C7+, Cdom7+	1,3,♯5,♭7
C half-diminished	Cmin7♭5, Cø	1,♭3,♭5,♭7
C diminshed7	Cdim7, C°7, C°	1,♭3,♭5,♭♭7

NINTH CHORDS		
C major 9	Cmaj9, C△9, CM9	1,3,5,7,9
C major add 9	Cadd9, Cmaj add9, CM add9	1,3,5,9
C half-diminished ♮9	Cm7♭5♮9, Cø♮9	1,♭3,♭5,♭7,♮9

SIXTH CHORDS:		
C major 6	Cmaj6, C6, Cadd6	1,3,5,6
C minor 6	Cm6, Cmin6, C-6, Cm add6, Cmin add6, C- add6	1,♭3,5,6

ELEVENTH CHORDS		
C major7♯11	C△♯11, Cmaj9♯11, CM9♯11	1,3,5,7,9,♯11
C minor 11	C min11, C-11	1,♭3,5,♭7,9,11
C half-diminished ♮11	Cm7♭5♮11, Cø♮11	1,♭3,♭5,♭7,9,11

EXTENDED DOMINANTS		
C dominant 9	C9, Cdom9	1,3,5,♭7,9
C dominant 9 suspended 4	C9 sus4, B♭/C	1,4,5,♭7,9
C dominant 7♭9	C7♭9, Cdom7♭9	1,3,5,♭7,♭9
C dominant 7♯9	C7♯9, Cdom7♯9	1,3,5,♭7,♯9
C dominant7♯11	C7♯11, Cdom7♯11	1,3,5,♭7,9,♯11
C dominant11	C11, Cdom11	1,3,5,♭7,9,11
C dominant13	C13, Cdom13	1,3,5,♭7,9,11,13
C dominant13 ♯11	C13♯11, Cdom13♯11	1,3,5,♭7,9,♯11,13
C altered	Calt, Calt7, C7♯5♯9, C7♯5♭9	1,3,♭5,♯5,♭7,♭9,♯9

N.B. *Be mindful that when using* alt *or* alt7 *as a symbol you are denoting a chord drawn from the altered scale and as such, implying that it can contain any combination of sharpened/flattened 5ths or 9ths, the choice of which is then up to the performer.*

INVERSIONS		
C maj 1st inv	C/E	3,5,1
C maj 2nd inv	C/G	5,1,3
C min 1st inv	Cm/E♭, Cmin/E♭, C-/E♭	♭3,5,1
C min 2nd inv	Cm/G, Cmin/G, C-/G	5,1,♭3

SCALES & MODES

Certain scales are often referred to in a variety of ways and as such, it is well worth becoming familiar with the terms below.

The following is a list of the modes of the major, harmonic minor and melodic minor scales. As you can see, some of these are expressed in a variety of ways and as such they are well worth familiarising yourself with.

MAJOR SCALE		
Ionian	Major scale, 1st mode of the major scale	1,2,3,4,5,6,7
Dorian	2nd mode of the major scale	1,2,♭3,4,5,6,♭7
Phrygian	3rd mode of the major scale	1,♭2,♭3,4,5,♭6,♭7
Lydian	4th mode of the major scale	1,2,3,♯4,5,6,7
Mixolydian	5th mode of the major scale	1,2,3,4,5,6,♭7
Aeolian	6th mode of the major scale, natural minor, relative minor	1,2,♭3,4,5,♭6,♭7
Locrian	7th mode of the major scale, Half Diminished	1,♭2,♭3,4,♭5,♭6,♭7

MELODIC MINOR		
Melodic Minor	1st mode of melodic minor	1,2,♭3,4,5,6,7
Dorian ♭9	2nd mode of melodic minor	1,♭2,♭3,4,5,6,♭7
Lydian Augmented	3rd mode of melodic minor	1,2,3,♯4,♯5,6,7
Lydian Dominant	4th mode of melodic minor	1,2,3,♯4,5,6,♭7
Mixolydian ♭13	5th mode of melodic minor, Hindu scale	1,2,3,4,5,♭6,♭7
Locrian ♮9	6th mode of melodic minor, half-diminished ♮9	1,2,♭3,4,♭5,♭6,♭7
Altered scale	7th mode of melodic minor, Superlocrian, Diminished whole-tone scale	1,♭2,♯2,3,♭5,♯5,♭7/1,♭2,♭3,♭4,♭5,♭6,♭7

HARMONIC MINOR		
Harmonic Minor	1st mode of harmonic minor	1,2,♭3,4,5,♭6,7
Locrian ♮13	2nd mode of harmonic minor	1,♭2,♭3,4,♭5,6,♭7
Ionian Augmented	3rd mode of harmonic minor	1,2,3,4,♯5,6,7
Dorian ♯11	4th mode of harmonic minor	1,2,♭3,♯4,5,6,♭7
Mixolydian ♭9, ♭13	5th mode of harmonic minor, Spanish phrygian, phrygian dominant, Jewish scale	1,♭2,3,4,5,♭6,♭7
Lydian ♯9	6th mode of harmonic minor	1,♯2,3,♯4,5,6,7
Ultralocrian	7th mode of harmonic minor, altered ♭♭7	1,♭2,♭3,♭4,♭5,♭6,♭♭7

TIME SIGNATURES

Although not a huge amount of options here, there are some often-used variations and definitions when it comes to expressing time signatures, in much the same way as the two commonly used systems for referring to note values. Again, there is nothing to be lost by committing these to memory.

4/4	Common time
2/2	Cut common, ¢, cut time
2/2, 2/4, 2/8	Simple duple
3/2, 3/4, 3/8	Simple triple
4/2, 4/4, 4/8, 4/16	Simple quadruple
6/4, 6/8, 6/16	Compound duple
9/4, 9/8, 9/16	Compound triple
12/4, 12/8, 12/16	Compound quadruple

INDEX

NOTES

FINAL THOUGHTS

Everyone involved in the creation of these texts has a passion and a talent for imparting crucial, industry-relevant knowledge, skills and experience, honed through countless hours of performing, researching and educating. When learnt, this knowledge will lead to more efficient practice sessions, more advanced skills and a deeper, more articulate understanding of popular music and its conventions.

These books are designed to give aspiring, modern musicians a structured approach to developing their theoretical knowledge, providing a strong foundation on which to build practical skills, whatever their area of specialism. At all points, care has been taken to provide a thoroughly engaging and rewarding experience in keeping with Rockschool's long-standing commitment to raising standards for the next generation of contemporary musicians.

John Simpson
CEO, Rockschool